Neurodivergent Voices Series:
GRIEF
Volume 1

Edited by Kit Caelsto

EPONA MUSE
PUBLISHING

COPYRIGHT

The scanning, uploading and distribution of this book via the Internet or via any other means without the permission of the publisher is illegal and punishable by law. Please purchase only authorized editions and do not participate in or encourage the electronic piracy of copyrighted materials. Your support of the author's rights is appreciated. Permission is granted to make ONE backup copy for archival purposes.

Contents

Introduction

Amazing things come from chance social media encounters. Someone mentioned wondering if there were any books on neurodivergent grief. A quick web search later, I realized there weren't many, if there were any at all. As someone with experience with putting together anthologies, I offered. Not only is this a topic of interest for me as I examine all the ways grief has touched my life, but I saw the project as a chance at public service, of putting my skills to use for the good of the neurodivergent community.

I am honored and humbled to be given the task of shepherding these essays into this volume. The stories told here are personal and moving. Grief, we're taught, moves in five phases: denial, anger, bargaining, depression, acceptance. Even in neurotypical spaces, the more compassionate and informed believe grief is a dance. It is not a linear movement through the stages. Some are skipped. Others are revisited. And even when we reach acceptance grief doesn't go away. It remains and theoretically lessens with time.

Neurodivergent grief, as told in these essays, also ebbs and flows through these phases, and just like neurotypicals we each grieve in our own way. I think it's important to note that we do grieve, and we grieve hard. The myth of the emotionless, almost robot-like autistic individual is just that—a myth and a purposefully wrong one as well.

Many scholarly articles have been written about rumination in autism, though it isn't until individuals actually talk with and listen to autistic individuals that it becomes clear a large part of rumination is the asking of "why?". The loss of friendships, pets, loved ones, jobs, or opportunities all cause grief. To the neurodivergent individual there's also the undercurrent of "why?" because too often we're left without answers as people, places, and things slip hopelessly, silently, out of our reach.

In this, grief becomes like the rubbing of salt in the wound, or picking off scabs, making the initial injury that much more difficult to handle. The sensory pain becomes too much, overwhelming, as the emotions flare. They do not go gently into the long night. Instead, they rage and recombine, showing themselves in new and sometimes raw and painful ways.

This anthology contains only a few essays of grief, and while I believe it gives a bountiful cross-section of the many ways grief manifests in our lives and how we handle it, this is by no means the entirety of the subject. We are human. We are as wondrous and varied as the leaves on the trees in a forest, and at times we're just as fragile.

To those who are neurodivergent, I hope this volume offers a light in the darkness, a way to begin to understand the ways grief shapes your life.

To those who are neurotypical, may you begin to understand us just a little bit more.

- *Kit Caelsto*

From Innocence to Closing Off to Self-Awareness to Rebirth: A Typical Autistic Tale, Unfortunately

by Jenny Bristol

Who were you before the world beat you down?

As I sit here, middle-aged and working on remembering and figuring out who I really am, I ask myself that question all the time. Who was I before society not-so-politely asked me to hide myself, hide who I really am? Who could I have been, if I'd been nurtured by society and my peers, instead of ridiculed and told I was doing things wrong?

I don't grieve over my autism diagnosis or a fictional self that I had built myself up to be. I've always known who I am, deep down, even without the words to express it.

No, instead, I grieve over the lost possibilities of my life and who I might have blossomed to be, given the right supports. Those lost possibilities are becoming evident as I unpack my several decades of undiagnosed life. For me, being diagnosed autistic was like focusing a camera lens, the blurry, mixed-up world finally becoming clear.

My entire life finally made sense. My weird behavior as a child. My awkwardness and rarely fitting in. My reactions to the world. My expectations of others. But the journey to reach this understanding was very long. And it was very short.

Learning I was autistic was a slow and gradual process, but then it happened all of a sudden, making it all feel obvious in retrospect, like I should have figured it out long ago. The long journey ended in a blip.

But it really was a long and complicated story, a folding and unfolding of the intricate layers of who I am and why I am this way. When I think about the long journey I took to get where I am today, I grieve for the unaffected, happy child that was lost in the sea of traumatic experiences, and am driven to uncover her again, to both continue my growth from where I am now, and to give her a chance to have all the experiences and growth she missed out on. But I'm getting ahead of myself. First, I need to make sense of my past.

Innocence

To get back to a time where I didn't use my autistic masks, I have to think back, further back, even further back.

I have to go back pretty far.

I think I was eight years old, the last time I truly felt free. I suppose I was lucky to make it that long.

I wasn't born into a place of trauma. My very early years were happy and felt secure. I was unaffected by the world, unaffected by ridicule, bullying, and more subtle microaggressions. This was before I turned inward and stopped being my full self with most people.

My life consisted of school and home, and lots of play. Most of my memories from school are of play, having recess and playing Four Square with my friends, climbing on the jungle gym, and so much jump rope. Home meant my mom, who was always my safe place, along with playing with the neighbor kids, dancing in the living room while my mom played piano, burning my hands making pull taffy in the kitchen, and eating sugar snap peas straight from the garden. My biggest tragedies were cutting off a bunch of my hair right before a friend's birthday party, or the typical bickering with my sister.

I was very good at being in the moment, enjoying what I was doing, and not worrying about most things. I could feel pure joy when I would swing on the swings. Or play a game. Or hunker down in a pillow fort. I wasn't as sensitive to the things going on around me, and if people thought I was weird, I didn't notice or internalize it. You can get away with a lot as a small kid, though, so that might have been part of it.

I felt like my real self and hadn't yet learned or been forced to hide who I was, editing my words and behavior for other people's convenience or for my own safety.

There were a few seeds of change from those early years, though. I do have a few memories from my early childhood where I experienced that my needs were different from those of other people. But when those needs were called out or ignored by others, they didn't yet affect how I interacted with the world. They were the exception rather than the rule and were isolated incidents.

First, I remember an incident in school. It was probably Kindergarten. I had brought a stuffed Woodstock (from *Peanuts*) to school one day. I kept him on a dog's leash, and I liked to swing him around at home. I swung him around in class that day, probably as a stim of some kind, and remember my teacher chastising me for doing that indoors, where I might hurt someone or break something. I felt very embarrassed for being called out in front of other students. I never brought Woodstock to school again.

Second was when my mom signed me up for swimming lessons. I was probably about seven. Our neighbor had a pool at their house, and their teenage daughter was giving lessons. Part of one lesson was to go underwater and open your eyes. I knew from experience that my eyes were really sensitive, and I didn't want to do that. I also knew that water would end up going up my nose. No one told me about goggles or nose plugs, and it was required that all students open their eyes under water to be able to progress. I couldn't. I wouldn't. The whole experience was traumatic, and I cried a lot. I think that caused me to quit the class, and it would be several years before I ended up teaching myself to swim (badly).

Third was probably my first indication (in hindsight) that things were changing for me. My school was having an art sale of sorts, and my mom and I were helping. I was wearing a pretty blouse that my mom had brought back from Colombia for me, where she was visiting my aunt, uncle, and cousins. A woman was photographing the event and wanted to take my photo. I didn't want her to. I was shy and didn't like to be the center of attention (not wanting to participate in Show and Tell at school had already taught me that). All of the adults were trying to talk me into letting her, but I cried and wouldn't let them. Then a man took over as photographer and basically didn't give me a choice, and I didn't feel I could say no at that point. My needs were ignored, even though I was communicating them clearly (even if I wasn't using full sentences to do so). I felt very exposed and a bit violated, and was quite upset that I was forced to do something I clearly wasn't comfortable with. But I was a little kid, and I didn't have the words to explain clearly and dispassionately. And people usually dismiss concerns brought up by little kids anyway. I think my mom was upset about me making a scene, but I don't blame her; I'm sure she was in an awkward position too.

Despite these isolated events, in between them I still felt safe and like I could be myself.

Turning Inward

When I was eight years old, things shifted. A whole lot happened that year: we moved to a new state, I got glasses and a weird haircut, and I think I "came into my own" as an autistic kid, becoming more aware of how people perceived me.

At school—from my peers, through bullying and othering and personal attacks—I was taught that who I really was wasn't acceptable. I got good grades and had curly hair, glasses, and teeth issues, and that was enough to be singled out. So, I retreated into myself, and only shared who I really was at home and with a friend or two (thank you, Sarah Miller, for being such a good friend for so many years).

Never along the way did I ever feel like part of a group. I always had a handful of usually individual friends, but never felt like part of something bigger while I was growing up. I was regularly excluded, often the last to be picked, even when I was good at something. I felt that I was on the outside, almost constantly. I wish I could go back in time and explain to Young Jenny just what was going on.

I spent much of my elementary school days dissociating, pretending like I wasn't really there, while still trying to pay attention and do the schoolwork. Sometimes while having to sit in the same desk area as my bullies. (I looked one of them up on the internet a couple of years ago—he had become a lawyer, but his practices were so shady that he had to change his name and flee the country!) I reveled in tetherball at recess, where I was really skilled, but most of the time I envisioned myself in a little bubble to protect me from the hateful and hurtful words tossed at me, just for looking and acting differently.

This continual abuse pushed me to be even more shy, even quieter, never asking questions in class even when I had them, never fully engaging with the material because I had to be on the lookout for external attacks.

As I grew, I slowly learned to adapt and navigate the tricky world of the neurotypical. I'd long forgotten about some of the ways I used to be when I was younger because I'd found workarounds or just suppressed those parts of myself. My good grades and consistent friendships probably made teachers think that I was okay, if a bit quiet. (Almost every parent/teacher conference consisted of, "She's doing great, with excellent grades, but I wish she'd participate in class more.") But autism wasn't something that many kids of my generation got diagnosed with, so I doubt my teachers were really looking for it. Frankly, I hadn't even heard of autism until I was an adult.

As time went on, I learned adaptations and accommodations for myself the hard way. I had no one to compare notes with. A book I read described being autistic as going through life on hard mode. Society just wasn't set up for people like me, but I still had to make my way through it and figure out how to survive, and to thrive if I could. In some ways I did thrive. In other ways, not so much.

I felt lost, like my brain didn't work fully. I could do math quizzes in no time flat, but when it came to understanding how I felt or how I should respond to a situation, I was lost. I felt immobile. Cloudy. Like I couldn't make sense of it.

I kept turning inward, not reacting to the bullying, not responding, but keeping it all inside. Living in fear. Going through my day anyway. I don't think I told my mom about the extent of the abuse I received at school. I don't know why I didn't tell her; maybe I didn't think she could help.

Instead, I spent a lot of time in my own head, where it was safe. I kept a lot inside, kept a lot to myself. But my exuberant personality was permanently affected, with me no longer sharing it except when I felt completely safe. Which was rare. I learned to create concentric circles of people, knowing who was safe and who wasn't, with only a select few in the inner circles. I should have been able to just be a kid.

I moved across the country again in junior high. At my new school, my peers kept up the constant abuse, keeping me from feeling safe expressing myself, to the point where I worked hard to muster up five outfits I knew wouldn't draw judgment or much attention. I wore those five outfits each week, keeping track of which day I wore which outfit, so I wouldn't repeat them too quickly. I wore clothes that reflected my own personal style and personality only on the weekends. I was otherwise too afraid of drawing attention to myself, too afraid of giving my bullies more ammunition for their attacks.

High school was considerably better, going to a nerdy science and tech school where most other people were misfits in some way too. But we were still teenagers, and I still didn't feel safe to fully be myself. I always had friends, but it took a lot of work to make connections with people. I do have some amazing memories from my high school years, but if I'd felt saver there could have been so many more.

In college, I felt like I lived in a bubble. I didn't live on campus and was shy in all my classes, so I had no college-based friends. I just floated from one class to the other, no one knowing me, me not knowing anyone.

A lot of the external pressure to not be myself went away after I graduated, but I never had a mentor or guide that could help me make up for the damage that had already been done. No one to help me figure out how to blossom into who I could be.

I was almost constantly in a relationship (two long-term ones overlapped my college years). While I felt I could be myself in the relationships in a few ways, both relationships were abusive. With my first one, I mostly just put up with it, because I'd been taught that it was normal for other people to not care about my needs, and for my needs to be minimized. Advocating for myself was something I hadn't quite mastered, and I felt that losing the relationship would have been worse than dealing with mistreatment.

With my second relationship, I did stand up for myself, but that created an environment of conflict, which was hard in its own way. When it became clear that he was not interested in growing as a person, I mentally checked out. I mourned that relationship long before it officially ended, to the point where I didn't shed a single tear for the loss after we split up, almost 17 years after the relationship had begun.

I was stunted at an early age and didn't have help coming out of it. I really only started coming into my own in my mid-30s, as the internet was taking off, as I reveled in parenthood.

It was such a relief when I had my daughter and could quit my job to stay at home with her at age 28, with my son following three years later. I finally felt like I could breathe. I felt like a huge weight had been lifted. I was barely holding it together having to work some weeks, and was definitely experiencing autistic burnout, though I didn't know it at the time. (I still carried other weights, such as my abusive marriage, but one thing at a time.) I even chose to homeschool them partly to prevent their education from being under the cloud of learning to be a survivor of abuse.

Even as an adult, I would occasionally be excluded for no given reason. Sometimes I found groups of people who included me and with whom I felt at home with. But, again, that was the exception rather than the rule. Especially socially. One time I formed a book club with some women I knew where we took turns choosing the book. A couple of books in, the club just stopped meeting, right after we read and discussed a book I had chosen. Or, rather, I thought the club had stopped meeting. In reality, the rest of them had just formed a "new" book club that didn't include me. These weren't my people, it turned out. I would have to find my people elsewhere.

Even people who loved me didn't understand me, but some of them tried, really hard. Others claimed to like or love me but were put off by my quirks and saw some of what I consider my strengths as faults. Some of them belittled me or tried to make me feel somehow less because of my (autistic) traits. They saw them as failings. My ex-husband even called me "broken" for not meeting some arbitrary standard. But I'm not broken. This is just how I am and how my brain works. In hindsight, others' behaviors told me more about them than about myself. Their behaviors told me to which of the concentric circles they belonged.

But I still didn't know why I was the way I was. I thought I was just weird, different from everyone else. I didn't have all the words for communicating my needs and identifying my missed experiences, missed opportunities for growth. I knew some of what was weighing on me, but I didn't know why.

Awakening

In my 40s, though, it all became clear. I had shed my abusive marriage, and found someone new who celebrated me, just as I was, in every way that I am. I could finally breathe.

My son was diagnosed autistic when I was about 40. I never thought he was autistic because he was just like me, and I thought I wasn't autistic. (A common tale.)

In the years that came afterward, I did a lot of research to find ways to help my son feel supported and to help him figure out who he was. The more I read, though, the more I wondered... hmm... "That sounds a bit like me." Or, "That sounds a *lot* like me." Lightbulbs were going off, left and right.

Since I'd only learned about autism as an adult, and only in the context of it being a problem, I found I had to edit a lot of my preconceived notions. I had to reframe what I thought about autism, understand asynchronous development, and connect with my kids and myself so deeply that I could pick up on our needs without struggling. My intense empathy helped with this task.

Additionally, autistic adults were starting to mobilize and congregate on social media, supporting each other, comparing notes, and realizing that many of the "deficits" of being autistic were because autistic people don't fit into a neurotypical society. Society wasn't designed by autistic people, or for autistic people. Reading about countless autistic experiences helped me realize that the truth lay in a different narrative. A narrative that autistic people were creating for themselves, rather than the one that was put on autistic people by those who pathologized autism, as if it were an illness or disease.

I felt it was imperative to learn how to best approach raising and teaching my son. But the more I read, the more it felt like I was looking into a mirror. The more things resonated with me. The more I felt that the books and articles were describing *me*. The me that didn't quite fit in with everyone else. The me that was othered. I learned that I wasn't alone in this "other" group. This realization, this gradual lifting of a weight, lifting of a veil from my eyes, lifting of an oppressive judgment that I'd carried with me for decades, caused me to keep digging.

This caused me to read more about autism with myself in mind. I took a plethora of notes about traits and behaviors of mine that could be considered autistic, which added up fast. I started re-examining past events in my life, actions I took, behaviors I exhibited, that I hadn't thought about in decades. Things I was teased about, things I tried to hide because people thought they were weird. And I looked at plenty of other things from adulthood, too. Most of these were described in the autism books I read, as experiences shared by other autistic people.

I felt like I was being pulled along, faster and faster, down a road of understanding. Pieces fell into place, one by one. Connections were made. Daily "eureka" moments were (and still are) experienced. I felt so many dissonant noises in my head that were all coming together, coalescing into one strong, clear, upward, triumphant note.

It became clear. I was autistic.

Or was I? Imposter syndrome is strong.

I started taking online autism tests. Some were pretty superficial, but others were more in-depth. They all said the same thing, that I have significant autistic traits but also a large amount of empathy. None of them clearly stated I was autistic, so I kept doubting myself. These were tests designed for males, though, so I did have to take it all with a grain of salt. But my hyper-empathy—along with my intelligence—is what has helped me mostly fit into the greater world, so it all started to make logical sense.

I then started reading books specifically on autistic women, and how different types of people often exhibit different autistic traits. More light bulbs went off over my head. Ping ping ping! An even clearer note sounded.

I had pages and pages of notes by this time, both from my readings and from my recollections. Very slowly, it felt like dawn was approaching. Like, wow, can this be for real? Was I right the first time? By the time the picture came into focus that I, too, was likely autistic, I felt so validated, and I finally felt free. It was such a relief to read about how I was probably not an anomaly in this world, that what I experience on a daily basis, and what I've rearranged my life to accommodate, isn't rare. It's common. It's just been vastly under-recognized, especially for women, and especially for people of my generation and older.

Three dense, well-organized pages of notes later, I decided I was definitely autistic late in my year of being 44. I had it confirmed by a psychiatrist soon thereafter at age 45. And my daughter was diagnosed soon thereafter. We still weren't sure about my partner because a lot of his traits could be attributed to various other diagnoses he had. (Spoiler: The more we all learned about autism, though, the clearer it became that he's autistic too. It just took us a few more years to get there.)

And there I was. I was autistic. I *am* autistic.

It felt like a destination, but really it was a beginning.

I dove in deep to autistic Twitter, Facebook groups, and other communities. I started writing about my experience and amplifying the voices of other autistic adults. I learned so much about people's experiences about being autistic, and what those who had been diagnosed younger had had to deal with. I learned about abusive "therapies" that cause PTSD. I learned about changing terminology.

And I became very grateful that I hadn't been diagnosed earlier.

If I'd been diagnosed as a child, I might have had more words to describe my experiences, but I probably would have internalized the negative messages from those who were supposed to help me and take care of me. My intelligence might have been discounted, and my "deficiencies" might have been the focus. I wouldn't have had the same educational opportunities that I did, because autism was seen (and is still seen, by so many) as a negative, a problem, a thing to fix.

I wouldn't have had decades of experience finding patterns in my own life to make sense of it all, and instead probably would have been told what to think. I wouldn't have had a community of other autistic people to talk to, people who have gathered together to learn from each other and advocate for themselves. I wouldn't have had the internet and social media to learn about autism from autistic people, and instead would have relied on books written by non-autistic people.

It was better to be in the dark about why I am the way I am than to internalize any negative perspectives from those in charge. No, I feel like I figured out I was autistic at just the right time.

But, as an inevitable part of looking back at my childhood and earlier life, finding patterns and realizing why I turned inward, a sense of grief descended, grieving the *me* that never had a chance to be. It wasn't clear to me at first; it was only after I sat with this new diagnosis for a while that I started to feel the depth of the loss.

Learning as a middle-aged female that I've been autistic all along, I finally have words for how I feel, how I act, and who I am. Labels can be so freeing and eye-opening; having the vocabulary to put my feelings into words, and to explain why I am the way I am, has been so empowering.

I re-evaluated... well... everything. My childhood, adolescence, and young adulthood. All of my romantic and other relationships. I was figuring myself out. I now knew why I respond so strongly to bad smells. Why others think I am being argumentative when I am just trying to gain clarification. Why I prefer to listen to familiar music. And why I can see the eventual result from almost any situation when others are blind to it.

Now that I understand myself so much better, and I'm looking back at my life, waves of sadness and grief overcome me sometimes, thinking about the me that remained undeveloped and unexplored, thinking about the me that was beat down by those around me and by society as a whole, thinking about the me that I could have become if only I'd had the right environment to thrive.

I'm still going through this mourning period—periodically interspersed with pushes of attempts at growth and rebirth—mourning the possibilities of what I could have become and what opportunities I missed out on along the way. I know who I am, but I learned that it wasn't safe to be that person with most people. So, I learned to hide it, and now it's my default to not be my full self. Fighting against that is an uphill battle, as trauma that shapes us in childhood is terribly strong and difficult to undo, even when you've made peace with it. On the one hand, I am greatly relieved to have not been diagnosed at an earlier age, as my current age and set of experiences provide perspective and confidence that I did not have in the past. But on the other hand, I did miss out on the opportunity of greater self-understanding at an earlier age. So, it continues to be a work in progress.

One of the more helpful things, for me, is to look at photos of myself from when I was a kid, adolescent, or young adult. I look at them, knowing who she is at that moment and who she is trying to be. Knowing who she is forced to be and who is aching to break free of constraints and instead be herself. I use that knowledge, those lost opportunities and loss of self, to fuel who I am trying to become now.

I use that when I interact online. I use that when I make new friends and interact with old ones. I use that when I am out in the world. Being middle-aged has helped me care less about what other people think, which has gone a long way to helping me be more myself and less concerned with how I come off to people.

It has also shed a bright light on all that I've missed, all that I've lost, all that never came to be. "Unrealized potential," as it were. I spent much of my childhood being bullied by peers and misunderstood by my family (they love me and they tried, and they get all the points in the world for trying).

I'm very good at a lot of things, but wasn't able to recognize or have recognized for me that those things that I'm good at were where I should spend my effort. How much would I have grown, how many skills would I have developed, if I'd just had a mentor or guide who could see in me the things that I couldn't? That society and my family couldn't (because no one understood any of this yet and no one had the words)?

I've figured out some ways to navigate society without everyone noticing that I don't fit in. Unless they look closely. It's a ridiculous amount of work for me. Certain "normal" aspects of life I've just had to give up, like a full-time job. I just can't keep up the energy level required for a regular job. This means I somehow find a way to live on very little money and have no idea how I'll manage in retirement. Though I grieve the lost relatively easy path to home ownership and financial stability, I still hold out hope that we can make it happen in a creative way, but I worry I will be too old to enjoy it.

Grieving the lost possibilities includes examining trauma snapshots from both childhood and adulthood, snapshots that make me want to go back in time and give

Younger Jenny a big hug. Such as the trauma I felt as a kid as I was bullied daily in school. The gaslighting and emotional abuse in romantic relationships. The being told I was broken when I knew I wasn't. The knowing that my traits which are odd and sometimes inconvenient are also invaluable strengths, both in interpersonal relationships and in the greater society, despite being told otherwise. My need to control my environment and being particular in certain things, now knowing that that means I know how to make myself feel more comfortable.

All of these things held me back, made me focus on surviving instead of thriving. They mostly killed my ability to experience joy. They ramped up my existing anxiety to an unhealthy level, causing me to choose what feels safe rather than what will make me feel more alive.

Blossoming/Taking Flight

All I can do is go forward from here. I may be almost 50, hampered by my complex PTSD from past traumas. I may have less time ahead of me than when I was young. But I'm trying to sort out the grief I feel for my lost opportunities of all kinds and figure out where to go from here and how to best make use of my next chapter, trying not to focus on wasted time.

I can use my newfound understanding of myself to make informed decisions, make plans, and communicate my ideas and needs to others. This involves very clear wordings, setting more boundaries for myself to protect my energy, and not feeling like I'm making my way in the dark. It's both exciting to know myself better, and depressing because of how long I've gone without knowing, how many poor decisions I've made. But it's impossible to live life 100% efficiently, so I'm also learning to forgive myself, to be kind to and gentle with myself. I'm putting in the work to understand myself and improve my inner monologue.

All we can do is start from where we are.

Fortunately, some others recognize my traits as strengths and cherish me as a friend or as family. Some even celebrate my weirdness. It is possible to be appreciated for who you are, one hundred percent. I've had relationships before that didn't nurture all sides of me. But for the past decade I've had a relationship where I am loved and cherished, precisely for my quirks and unusual traits. The same traits that annoy other people are appreciated and found useful now. I've never felt so validated in my life. *I've always known that I'm interesting and amazing and intelligent* (thanks, Mom, for all the validation!), but I knew that others often didn't recognize it, and I turned inward to protect myself. Now, though, I work very hard at not caring what other people think and realizing that the people who don't appreciate me aren't worth my energy. There are so many other people who are.

This environment of complete freedom, support, and acceptance was what I needed to successfully re-examine my life, talk it out, and rediscover who I am, and to find all of the parts that may have been misplaced along the way. There is complete non-judgment for my mistakes and missteps because they are all seen in the context of my life, experiences, and strengths. This shift has allowed me to start seeing parts of myself more clearly than I ever had before, my reasons for why I do the things I do and feel the things I feel.

Now that I can see myself in an autistic context, I work hard to remember who I was before I started hiding many of my traits from the world. It's an ongoing process, but one which is already buoying my sense of self. It's a matter of changing my perspective.

My next chapter, once my kids are both independent, will be to fully embody the person I knew I always was inside. To experience things that I was too scared to do, because previous traumas told me it wasn't safe. To be more of my full self with more of the world.

Some examples include: Wearing clothes that I love but might draw attention to me. Speaking up more in groups. Being bolder with sharing my opinions and ideas. Being visibly sillier and following my stream of consciousness more. Taking up space, both physically and metaphorically. Being okay with not everyone liking me, since the people who will like me for all my self-expression will like the *real* me.

I'm using my grief and mourning for the lost aspects of my life to inform future decisions and live a life that feels more "me" than ever before. I'm using my waves of understanding, epiphanies, and joys to figure out where I thrive. This is both hampered by and informed by so much regret, mourning, and grief over a missed life and missed opportunities, but I am working hard to make sure these turn into new opportunities and motivations.

I want to do more of the things that bring me joy and bliss. I want to swing on swings. I want to lose myself in my family history research. I want to explore new areas, see new sights, smell new smells, taste new tastes. I want to write more books. I have ideas for so many more books.

I want to be my full self, unhindered by messages I've received in the past telling me that I'm not allowed to be who I really am.

I want to be who I really am.

Now is *my* turn to fly. I'm doing it for Young Jenny. I'm doing it for Future Jenny. I'm doing it for me.

About the Author

Jenny Bristol is an author and freelance writer who seeks out unique experiences and interesting people wherever she goes. She is also an autistic advocate, Editor-in-Chief of the geeky parenting blog GeekMom.com, and parent to two incredible autistic adults. Jenny is a Gen-Xer who was diagnosed autistic at age 45 and has been having a series of lightbulb moments ever since, finally understanding her entire existence. You can find her at jennybristol.com or buy her books on Amazon at https://amzn.to/3i2xhfS.

The Shell Will Tell You Everything: A Nonlinear Story of Grieving

By Irisanya Moon

When I was young, I remember going to my mother and telling her that I thought the Challenger explosion I saw in class was beautiful. Her face was horrified, and I didn't know what was wrong.

"People died," she said.

Realizing my mistake, I quickly fixed my face and tried not to remember the colors that attended the destruction. But even today, I can see them in my mind.

My brain has always been a funny thing when it comes to horrors and loss. I dance with them because I know these moments to be the most authentic. They are places of connection and creativity. They are places where I really know myself and know that I can feel and care and love.

Grief is funny. So are humans. From the time we are young, we are asked what is wrong. Not what we are feeling. There has to be an explanation first. There has to be a reason. There has to be something that we did wrong or felt wrong because we wouldn't be sad or mad or whatever inconvenient feeling we're expressing for any other reason.

I wish it were different. I wish we would stop pointing at grief and those who grieve as ones to worry about. I wish we could look to them to see what is true. That we could sit by their side, listen, and learn how deep love runs. That we could stay by their side, not offering condolences or platitudes, but rather presence.

When my mom died, the first thing I did was reach out to people to be by my side. I didn't want to talk about anything. I just wanted to not be alone with my feelings and the way they were already crashing against the shore of what I knew. What I thought I knew. I was already dissociated and distant, clinging to the words that I only partially heard in the background.

I paced in the backyard. I walked from one end to the other while a friend waited with me, listening to all of the things I wanted someone to take care of. I had things I was responsible for, and I couldn't let anyone down. Even if my mother had died. (Maybe even especially then.) After all, I didn't dare do anything that might cause me to lose one more person.

Not now. Not ever.

I was outside of my body and inside of the places that rumble when they are agitated in any way. I was lost in the unknown place that I had not prepared for, that I did not have a list for, that I did not ruminate about at night until all of the things I needed to do were burned in my memory long before they met paper.

It would take years of therapy to get to the place where I was upset about my mom in a way that felt real. I was too competent at putting on a mask that looked right from the outside but itched from the inside. I was too tired from holding it all in that I would collapse as soon as I was out of eyesight. As soon as I was behind a door no one could open. As soon as I could. Away. Away.

And I also knew what grief looked like. I knew what it was supposed to do when out in public. The sadness and the sad looks and the slow movement from one place to another. I knew not to be too joyful, lest anyone think you didn't care enough. In my daily life, I was sad enough to be acceptable but not so sad that people would worry.

But I was worried. I didn't know what to do with all of these feelings. They poured out of me in poems. They flowed from my mouth with the few people who would listen. And all of that still didn't smooth the edges grief was making in the shape of my body. I felt the roughness. The pain. The slow.

I didn't deal with it. I decided that time would take care of all things. That I just needed to wait it out, outrun it. I just needed to do everything so that we didn't have to talk about it too much. I would go back to teaching two weeks later. Teach in Europe a few months later. I would take on new projects and new commitments like they were life jackets, when really, they only kept my head above water.

You can breathe above water. So long as I was doing that, I would be okay. So long as I could breathe, I could make it to the far-off time when I wouldn't have to feel this anymore. I could hyperfixate and breathe until then.

But grief comes with companions. This life does not stop because of loss. It continues toward the places where you can lose more and more and more. It shows you that there is always more to lose. A beloved friend. A relationship. Another parent.

You will lose them all. Eventually.

What I have learned is not simple or even new. It is only gathered and believed when you have lost enough to know you will not be spared. No matter what your brain says, it cannot stop what is coming. And going. And leaving and dying every single moment.

Listen to it.

Sit by the shores of grief and let the waters hit your feet.

Let the water carry you a little bit, enough to know you were never steady to begin with.

There is no right way to feel. There is no right way to be when the emptiness arrives. When the goodbyes are said -- or missed. You just need to be there.

You can pace in the backyard. You can sob in the middle of Costco. You can drive until the dawn catches up with you. You can hide. You can scream. You can surround yourself with distractions. You can numb yourself with whatever calms you this time.

You can do all of this. And grief will still find you.

Let it.

You will know yourself in your sharp pain of aliveness. In the beat of your heart. Still going. Still going on.

You will not lose yourself. And even if you do (for a moment or ten), you will return. Grieving is as natural as breathing and as frequent.

You will grieve a thousand times today. Tomorrow. In your bedroom. In the bathroom. At a drugstore. When you're having coffee. You will grieve because it is everywhere and everyone.

Let yourself close your eyes, touch your chest, and drop your shoulders.

If you hold a shell to your ear, you can listen to the ocean of your mind. The waves, the whooshes. And the wisdom of being quiet enough to hear your heartbeat back to you from a curve of creation.

And it might be horrible. And it can be beautiful.

About the Author

Irisanya Moon (she/they) is an author, witch, international teacher, and Reclaiming initiate who has practiced magick for 20+ years. She wrote 7 books (so far), including Pagan Portals (Reclaiming Witchcraft - 2020, Aphrodite - 2020, Iris - 2021, Norns - 2023), Earth Spirit (Honoring the Wild - 2023, Gaia - 2023), and Practically Pagan: An Alternative Guide to Health & Well-being - 2020. Irisanya cultivates spaces of self-care/devotion, divine relationship (whatever that means to you), and community service as part of her heart magick and activism.

Three Essays of Predominantly Autistic Grief
By Zuleima, neurodivergent researcher

Story 1: canine companions forever

My first loss was Bruno. He was ill and spent the night out in the garden, probably in pain and confused. Not my choice, my parents were/are cruel to the core. I said goodnight, and I knew he will not see me tomorrow. I was the first awake. There he was, still and stiff, surrounded by a little bit of fog and frosted grass. I walked towards him, and he was stiff and cold. He was dead. I do not remember anything else afterwards.

More dogs came and went. But one another is strong in my chest and memory. Her name was Pupis. She was a stray and knew how to smile showing her teeth. She was loyal to the core. But she got cancer and a surgery for it. She would not rest, and I think that my mother murdered her by manslaughter. She may have paid and made a great effort to have her tumour removed surgically, but what came next was manslaughter. Instead of dutifully caring for her and supervising her movement to promote healing of the skin at the sutures, my mother continued her routine, and we went out, somewhere I do not remember. But I remember coming back and strongly hoping that Pupis would stay laying down resting in her den instead of coming to the front door to greeting us full of energy as she always did. Unfortunately, she was there, and the sutures were broken. Internal organs hanging.

I despised my mother for this. She took her on the back of the car and did not give me a chance to say goodbye. I thought she was going to take her to fix her, but instead she took her and did not bring her back. I lost her and I did not say goodbye. I am looking forward to seeing her again, hug her and tell her that I am sorry for what she went through, and that I love her.

The most recent dog I lost is Pantera, my grandmother called me to tell me she died. I felt sad and a knot in my throat. It was sadness because I wanted more time with her but our respective lifetimes had not match well. She was living in Mexico with my grandmother and I was in London doing the work-living routine. Last time I saw her I said goodbye to her as if I would never see her again. I felt her tiredness and heaviness. I told her "I love you and I will miss you". When I think of her my forehead and eyebrows contract a little and some water accumulates in my eyes. But not enough to throw some lagrimas (eyedrops). Her fur was all deep black and soft, a mix of Labrador with something else, kindest eyes, carried herself with endless assertiveness, wagged the tail. Her signature movement was sitting on my feet while resting her body against my legs and raising her head to do eye contact with me. Her eye contact did not hurt. Feeling each other was our language.

Does anyone else prefers and is keen in eye contact with dogs in comparison with humans? I do. Nowadays I am accompanied by Bombon, he is a mixed breed and a rescue, he is also my assistance dog. Together we get through each day of this life and death existence. For however long we have left. Maybe one day we can both go to sleep hugging each other and together die, in peace and with our bellies full of a tasty dinner.

Story 2: kisses, always

My cousin called me, and he said that my grandfather had died. He was not crying. He was sobbing, and I felt his pain, his loss. But I was not in pain. I could not understand why and how he was not ready for this. I was calm, and I knew this was coming. I think that I felt comfort knowing that my grandfather was no longer having pain in his hip, frustration with not being able to walk as he wanted, aggravated by the medicine he knew he should take but always felt contempt to take and the endless boredom of everyday that was over. I saw his depression symptoms and his denial of treatment. I did not mention this to my cousin, how could I? He was hurting so much. I was only able to offer him support. I still have not been able to cry. I feel no need to. I am not saying that I do not care, which is typically what neurotypical would say. On the contrary, I care, but I understand this and expected this. I am not afraid of death and as a Mexican, I know death is coming, and I think of it every day. I even celebrate it (Day of the dead). To provide context, indigenous groups in what is today Mexico would have and show respect and admiration to life and death. Mexicans are not obsessed with death nor have a morbid attitude to it. I like that death is not hidden away in Mexico. It is visible, talked about and even joked about. I see death as a natural process and accept it, expect it. I do not feel contempt towards death. Instead, I am mindful of it. But being mindful of death can only be achieved by being mindful of life also. I requested my cousin to help me speak with my grandmother. He recommended the best time and I called. I was keen in the details, what time and what was he doing. So I could imagine his death and remember it. I have the feeling that this is a cultural thing. But I am not sure since I have not asked others about this to compare expectations of information regarding the death of a loved family member. Then, as a predominantly autistic human, I think of death more often and desire for it daily. There is no day I feel worthy, enough, happy with what I am and where I am. I hate the dominant neurotypical human species far too often. Verbalizing this would probably have me isolated much more, even writing it here, too much? I envy my grandfather's death, but I do not want to have to grow older to die. I want death earlier.

In the days following the call of my cousin I wrote a social media thread for my grandfather. Here is a copy of it. The title is "A mixed language tribute thread about my grandfather", because, of course, I speak Spanish and

English, so it is perfectly reasonable to feel emotions in two languages:

He was my father figure

He checked on me often:

1. ¿Te vas guapa al trabajo?

2. Viste bien eh!

3. ¿Cómo estas hija?

4. Te quiero mucho hija

5. Tu eres buena

6. Buenos días amor

7. Besitos para ti amor siempre

8. Buenos días hija, que tengas bonito día

9. Besitos

He said "I do not need a scooter"

I brought one from the UK to Mexico

I did not tell him

I put it on the boot of a small Yaris, three buses, one airplane and the back of a truck

He decorated it with tools and what not

He added a cushion at the basket for Nube

(Nube is a little white female fluffy dog)

He took the scooter around the garden y en la cocina de humo

But he did not need it

Or that is what he thought

Le gustaban los tamales y el atole

Como a mi

Le gustaba la barbacoa con consome y los pasteles

Como a mi

Le gustaba el mole y el queso asado

Como a mi

Pero le gustaba mas todo lo que mi abuela cocina

Como a mi

He grew up poor y estudió hasta tercero de primaria para trabajar

Pero a mi me mando a la Universidad

Me enseñó a no tener deudas

I told him "I am autistic" but it made no difference

He loved me the same

Se fué con un tamal verde y atole de fresa

Gracias

Besitos

Siempre

When I think of my grandfather, I feel affectionate and warm. He was what he could be and tried his best to be there for me as best as he could in the only way he knew he could. I can work and take care of myself today thanks to him and my grandmother. My grandmother is next, and I do not know how I will feel about her death, but I know that it is coming. I hope that it is peaceful, like my grandfather's, and I hope that when she is gone that I have an additional strong reason enough to be here in this world, because as soon as my assistance dog is gone, I will go, too. I am glad that she has her grave purchased and the funeral services arranged. She is ready, but she is happy living whatever she has left.

Story 3: grieving my own life

This type of grief is more difficult to unravel because it is compounded with trauma. This type of grief consists in the hypothetical life I could be living if I had known at an earlier age that I am neurodivergent. I am filled with a heavy feeling of grief, disappointed over the traumatic events that I had to live through, that I hopelessly lived through, not knowing that I was manipulated or abused or infantilized or considered inadequate or inappropriate. I am exasperated by dreams where I relieve traumatic events that I could have prevented or handled better. To protect myself from further trauma. Some days I wake up irritated and disgusted by the neurotypical human species. The nights that I have no dreams are the good ones. I am eager to have more dreamless nights.

About the Author

Zuleima is neurodivergent, predominantly autistic and intersecting ADD, dyslexia, dyscalculia, and dyspraxia. But she/they not always knew this is, in itself, a cause of grief. Honestly, I do not like to write biographies because these assume that were are static and we are not. We change with time and who I describe today will not be the same later. Maybe I will be a better version or a careless one. I do not know.

Website:
https://zuleimamorgado.wixsite.com/zuleimaresearcher

Rituals of Grief
by Grace O'Malley

I came to this anthology not as a scholar or scientist, like so many of our contributors, but from my own rigorously tested belief system. I am, in fact, a priest. New Moon priestess of a polytheist coven, to be clear, a duly elected High Priestess to others, and ordained minister to a small community. I am also a terminally online, technology-sodden acolyte of the fastest-moving information age in history. I have watched, observed, and integrated fully hundreds of our rapidly evolving rituals around grief literacy into my own practices. Human grief is no mystery to those of us who have lived through countless ends-of-the-world until today, is it? In the ages between the discovery of those first Neanderthal ritual burials, that six-foot axe priestess with the golden eye, those myriad vampires buried under Eastern European crossroads, all the way through the present day, where we spent a good portion of 2019 imploring archaeologists via Twitter shitpost to let us drink the sarcophagus juice, we have spent hundreds of years dissecting the rituals of societal, familial, and communal mourning.

Still, where I write about experiences within my own personal context, it will always be that of a person responsible for constructing those rituals and teaching others. It is my belief that above all other decree of any religion comes the task of joining in community with one another. The tasks of vulnerability, caring, and extending support are given by nearly every holy writing in human history. So many of us, as neurodivergent people, never experience that deep love in a world that does not consider our needs quite as "real" as those of the neurotypical. When it does come to us, often it comes with struggle, or at the cost of the energy required to mask. So, we build our own communities, our own societies. And like any society throughout history, we have begun to construct our own traditions and rituals around transitional events. This one, specifically, death, grief (whether personal or collective), and mourning, whether with our neurotypical loved ones or in the company of other neurodivergent folks, is one of the most visible. We are not invited into every transitional experience of community life, but the death of an individual in this peculiar modern day always shows the gaps in the weave we have so carefully constructed. Whether we call it religion, spirituality, philosophy, or faith, sincere belief can act as a solid core for further examination of this issue among many others.

This is not really self-help, a checklist, a recipe–please understand I offer the beginnings of a framework for you to build upon in your own meaningful ways. Take tactics and knowledge from your own lived experiences, your community, and your traditions; swap things in or out as needed. It's not only respectful for you to do so, I consider it a vital part of contributing to that very weave of education, understanding, and responsibility, with empathy. Thank you for the work you've already done for yourself and others by seeking more ways to understand and support your brain! Before I really get started, I want you to sit for a moment with this:

Neurodivergent people, you, your loved ones, and I—we have been compelled to become experts on our own experiences, whether it's rooted in trauma, alienation, ineffective or overly-effective coping mechanisms. We're building together and learning from each other every day, no matter how alone you feel. You have already taken unimaginable steps to connect with others without resorting to masking your brilliant neurodiverse self. I think that's incredible.

We're going to go through a few different topics today, from the basis of rituals surrounding grief, some specific things you may want to look up after (or in conjunction with) reading this book, and my specialty: learning to access your own grief through constructed ritual and ways to build them for your own particular needs.

When we were young, we were given maps and guidelines to make our way in a neurotypical world. Our understanding of our own brains can sometimes recall those stories and myths of mazes, of labyrinths and spells, while we grow and learn. A neurodivergent person can present in any number of ways, but a common thread is often the alienation of dissimilarity, a nagging hangnail sense of incomprehensible difference that leads to acting out, to masking, to self-judgment, negativity, even trauma. In the stories we tell our children, it is the *special* character or a different, more clever, less-worldly person who always comes out on top. Who triumphs over the evil, or the greedy, or simply over those beholden to more socially acceptable behavior or beliefs. As we age, we no longer are expected to identify with the clever princesses or wise magical creatures or foolish third sons, but instead, to become the kings, viziers, wise farmers, comfortable and incurious townspeople. It is a dissonance that creates a tension in some neurodiverse people; we are and will remain the "different."

There are many, many places we thread our way through understanding ourselves. So how do we reconcile that difference with the common human longing to connect? Many times, we find ourselves listing the ways neurodivergent people are failed by their communities and surrounding structures, and it can definitely be a way to connect, as well as validate one another, while we are unpacking those maladjusted coping skills we have evolved to merely survive the onslaught of neurotypical expectation. Still, responding to those who have failed us (even without malice), does not always satisfy. In a world made for the comfort and accommodation of neurotypical brain function, what if we instead sought ways to allow the neurotypical person to work within *our* frameworks and needs? They may not consciously comprehend the solidity and care of our desires and abilities, but our contributions can enrich *them* rather than bring more stress to *our* lives. It may help you to be reminded that grieving is a type of *learning*, something we're uniquely suited to. Many of us expend hours, days, years upon learning, even focusing on it to a degree and with an excitement for simple knowledge that neurotypical people find alluring but difficult to understand. More than any *tradition* or *expected performance* of grief or mourning, we often seek instead accuracy of information, facts, honesty, inclusion, and *consistency*. In this context, just as any other search for genuine and comprehensive inclusion of the neurodivergent mind, we want to build a framework for the event that is both made for and by other neurodiverse. We also may need more time to come to terms with our loss or explore the meaning of our own grief than someone assumed to be neurotypical. Remember that our entire written history (not just of mourning and the rituals surrounding these transitional events of death, loss, disconnection) has been recorded by people who research with the assumption that there is a "normal" way to do these things–an assumption of basic similarities due to the commonality of the neurotypical experience.

Your example of, and your experience with neurodivergent grief may be completely different from mine. However, we can utilize our deep capacity for empathy not just to relate to one another as neurodiverse, but to bring that empathy and care to the neurotypical so that we do not make the mistake of shutting them out of community as has so often been done to us. We strive to not just *acknowledge* but *honor* our differences in the construction of this framework–one where we can dispense with masking or the stress of accommodating neurotypical thought, and yet still remain in community with our neurotypical friends, family, and allies. This is vital to comprehending and validating our own neurodivergent brain function, to becoming comfortable in our unmasking, to healing from trauma. Remember, in fairy tales and folklore, it is the *different* child who triumphs, and in our lives we can taste the same joy, even in sorrow.

So, let's set out on that folkloric path into the woods where the monsters wait. Many neurodiverse people find themselves coping with a neoclassical Hydra when it comes to grieving. Each problem, overwhelming in its own right, can spawn new problems from each solution! We'll start with a common complaint. You have suffered a loss of any size–how was grief modeled for you as a child? Often, we encounter difficulties in our attempts to access our particular methods or styles of grieving because what we learned to be the "correct" way to mourn doesn't suit our specific needs. Whether it's a personal or communal grief, our communities may have standards that are perfectly comfortable for the neurotypical brain, and since those were the models we learned to be appropriate, we begin receiving yet another message of unworth due to our inability to connect those standards with our needs. Add to this someone's sensory needs or issues, and you'll see that we can unwittingly be barred from the very traditions that lead the neurotypical to a catharsis. Even worse, the stages of grief so commonly accepted by the neurotypical world can frustrate or alienate a neurodivergent person who finds them disorderly or outside their own experience. Neurodivergent people often find themselves in the unenviable position of independent grieving or having to craft their own access to or relationship with grief from whole cloth. The ability or obligation to cherry-pick familial tradition in order to model a grief for yourself that makes sense and allows you to experience the same function of healing is sometimes overwhelmed by the expectations of the neurotypical, adding yet *another* undeserved burden. This can lead to further tension and masking, even by someone working hard to comfort themselves and others though they have not yet figured out a way to touch their own grief.

Independent grieving, whether due to estrangement, lack of familial or community understanding, or an inability/lack of desire to access or honor social convention, sounds like a tough business. Still, it can allow us to establish good boundaries with ourselves and others while we continue the work of acknowledging and healing from the forced masking many of us must still perform. It allows us to assign value to the relationships as we choose. For example, a personal relationship or a community relationship may take precedence over a familial one. This does not divest us from the familial relationship; instead, it allows us a clearer understanding of our own desires and boundaries and so supports our healthy interaction with the "typical" neurotypical family.

There's been loads of research done on patterns of grief and styles of mourning, and while I will touch on some of it, it's important to bear in mind that this research (like everything else) assumes neurotypical brain capacity, so we'll touch on a few previously recognized topics merely to begin building your own place to stand. With that in mind, having the language to strengthen your capability for frame-building may assist you in deciphering commonalities with your own relationship to grief. An easy place to begin your search are the three currently recognized patterns or styles of grieving. We call them "instrumental," "intuitive," and "dissonant."

The "instrumental" griever often utilizes information or physical fact to remain detached and dispassionate in the face of their grief. "Intuitive" grievers can appear overwhelmed by their emotions but are, ironically, comfortable with the strength of the feelings while they experience the full range of their grief without attempting to rationalize the deeper feelings away. Meanwhile, the "dissonant" griever appears to have a major conflict between the experienced emotion and the expression of it, which can lead to conflicts either within themselves or their community. One way dissonant grief is performed is self-condemnation or guilt for *not* performing their grief as "expected."

A neurodivergent person has experienced aspects of all three of these neurotypically common styles at least once in their life while being forced to deal with the repercussions of operating in a neurotypical society! So we are, in fact, well-suited to describing, framing, and creating spaces and rituals for others in times of need. When we acknowledge this as a strength, rather than judging ourselves for not performing like a neurotypical person, the hydra of our stress may lose its ability to overwhelm. So how can we turn those fears into positive reflections?

First, by being aware of our own style of grief; by seeking clear and concise knowledge of our community or familial relationship to mourning ritual; by giving ourselves the grace to take whatever time is needed to access the grief while holding firm and loving boundaries; by leading with empathy; and finally, by eschewing masking that we may instead offer the honest and deep experience of mourning to our families or communities. Our senses and sensory needs, in conjunction with all these lessons, can provide a sturdy framework on which we can trust ourselves to hang the carefully woven offering. Each time we craft a small ritual to honor our own interior landscape, we become more confident in connecting with neurotypical loved ones or fellow neurodiverse people without resorting to masking. We can use the same practices to construct routines and rituals for cathartic mourning.

Let's step off the path–I brought some breadcrumbs to mark the safest path home, and I want to show you what I found when I began to look for mourning in my own heart:

I have a hangnail, a torn cuticle on my right thumb that annoys me every time I remember its presence, and this, to me, is the easiest metaphor for grieving. It is a piece of me that does not care for my needs or desires; it simply exists to catch on everything, to hurt and bleed, to stick out when I rub my finger over the tip of my thumb, and my only solutions for that are to ignore it until it heals, leaving it alone–which I cannot do–or pick at it compulsively–which I cannot stop. It does not matter to the soft animal of my body that I cannot grip the loose end with my teeth; I am still trying.

But we are here, brought together by the universal human desire to make sense out of loss. Many threads of ritual have come from that ageless need; the one that speaks most strongly in me is the longing to succor the living. I'm descended from the kind of people who won't send flowers to a funeral but will leave a casserole on your porch to save you the effort of hearing more condolences. I wrote the above paragraph just a week or two before this essay was due, when I lost my final living grandparent. Even while I was crying at the news that I would not, as I had hoped, be able to see him before the end, I was laughing and cussing that old man for providing me with such painful insight on the topic. Eventually, when the most volatile emotions had passed, I found myself struggling to access some way to mourn him, even though I am estranged from my family. I had no traditional way to show my grief or to expiate that loss without contacting our shared relatives, and my boundaries are such that I do so infrequently and at great cost to myself. While considering all the things my grandfather meant to me, I was struck by the comfort I remembered in shared meals and the love he showed in cooking and with food. My body made the decisions for me, unburdened by community expectations; I spent the day of that first flush of grief preparing a *major* meal, adding to family recipes and changing some of my own to reflect aspects of the love I felt in those days. This couldn't make the grief recede, become healed or immediately expected. In fact, I could barely eat anything I had prepared by the time it was ready to serve. But by turning the kinder memories, the memories full of love and value into something *tangible*,

I was able to offer up my love of–and grief for–my grandfather as a meal for the friends and family I have now, who were unable to meet him or love him as I have, fiercely, all my life.

Inside your own memories and our shared human desire are these same threads, warp and weft. I would like to invite you into the garden of that mythical gingerbread cottage, just before the turn towards the castle on the hill surrounded by an enormous briar hedge. Let's weave together and mount it on the framework of all these understandings.

In order to craft a ritual, in any religion or path, you begin with desire. A desire in this grieving ritual might be to honor that person you have lost. This framework will work with any grief or loss, and, as always, you are restrained only by the limits of your own imagination. I offer the barest bones for you to make into something as ornate or subtle as your path determines. Historically, humanity has offered grave goods, including funerary meals as well as farewell music, art, dancing, or even symbols of themselves to accompany the dead along their journey. In building your ritual, consider the focused desire–above, we determined to honor our lost soul. One way to do so is to drink a final toast to that person. You may choose to light candles, to contact others and plan to all raise a glass at a coordinated time, or to cook a family dinner. Whatever you choose to create based upon your love and grief, regardless of what someone else may think, will always be the right thing when made with the genuine desire to remember and to honor your dead. Here is a simple and customizable ritual to build upon:

You will need a large tumbler, glass, mug, or other drinking implement, a candle, a comfortable and safe place to perform this ritual, and ideally a picture or some item that brings your loss clearly to your mind. You may utilize whatever prayers, poetry, proverbial sayings that spark a connection, or you may work in silence.

Fill your glass with the liquid of your offering. For example, the memory of my grandfather is always a memory of the scent of a light beer with his strong hugs–I do not drink beer, so while I used a can of beer in the braise I made with dinner specifically for that reason, I chose simply to use water in my offering glass. Light the candle and speak whatever prayer feels appropriate to ask the universe to bear witness to the memory of your loss. Breathe deeply while contemplating the picture and focusing completely upon your desire to honor this person and commend their soul or memory to your preferred destination. Speak again, even if it is in the silence of your mind, to tell the lost soul that you are present and full of love and gratitude for their memory, and bow your head respectfully. Take the offering-cup in both hands, raise it to the candle and picture, and toast. You may close with another memory or prayer in that person's name, and bow your head again while visualizing as firmly as you can embracing that person farewell or watching them move on to their destination, with all the love you can evoke. You may choose to carefully snuff the candle and keep it, lighting it to repeat this routine as often as the grief rises in a new wave. You may choose to allow the candle to burn itself out in memory of the lost one. This ritual can be expanded upon if you must plan a funeral service or can be simplified in any way that makes it yours.

We are all connected in the simple human desire to remember and be remembered, and whatever shape that takes in your community or family tradition, you may also take the opportunity to connect with our history, our future, or simply your desire to know that what you have lost continues on–and for that, I can offer only three things. Following this essay, you will find recipes, one for a formerly traditional "West Virginia Funeral Cake," one of which could be found in the hands of at least one of my ancestors to leave on the kitchen counter while they tidied up around your house without any conversation, mouth set and jaw firm but never weeping, although they might have admitted to something in their eye, if y'all were close. You will also find a historical recipe for a "Parting Glass," though considering the ingredients I make no claims of authenticity other than it is a very Appalachian sort of mix–Italian, Irish, Scottish, African-American, English...and both hills and holler.

Secondly, whether you are of a mystic or scientific bent, you may hold this in your heart against despair in grief: the law of conservation of energy states that within a system, such as our universe, no energy can ever be created nor destroyed, only changed, transformed, or transferred from one form to another. No one is ever really gone, and nothing you lose is ended.

Finally, a blessing, if you'll have it–that in your heart you find grief transmuted into grace, that your loved ones understand they are loved forever, that you prosper, seek your truth, and gain a deeper understanding of your abilities not only in grief, but other strong emotions, while honoring all the effort you've put into yourself to make it here. May we always move in the direction of a better world.

West Virginia Funeral Cake (Traditional)

Yields one 9" square cake.
1 stick butter
2 tablespoons cocoa powder
1 cup granulated sugar
1 teaspoon baking soda
1 egg, beaten
¼ teaspoon ground cinnamon
1 capful good vanilla extract
¼ teaspoon ground cloves
1 cup all-purpose flour
1 cup buttermilk

Preheat oven to 350 degrees Fahrenheit. Grease a 9" square cake pan.

Cream butter and sugar together until fluffy. Add egg and vanilla. Sift together in a second bowl the flour, cocoa, spices, and baking soda. Add this to the egg mixture a little at a time, alternating with the buttermilk, and stir until smooth. Scrape batter into prepared pan and bake from 30-35 minutes or until a knife inserted into the center comes out clean.

For the frosting:
1 stick butter, melted
⅔ cup cocoa powder
3 cups powdered sugar
⅓ cup milk
1 capful good vanilla extract

Mix butter and cocoa in a large bowl. Add milk and sifted powdered sugar alternately to the cocoa mixture. Beat well until it comes to a spreadable consistency and add vanilla last.

If the frosting gets too thick, add more milk a little at a time until you like it better. Spread this frosting on the cake while it is still warm, and take it to the grieving family–or serve with funeral sandwiches after the viewing.

A "Parting Glass," after the early Scottish song first recorded in the Skene Manuscript between 1615 and 1635:

"But since it fell into my lot that I should rise and you should not

I'll gently rise and softly call, 'Good night and joy be with you all.'

Fill to me the parting glass and drink a health, whate'er befalls

Then gently rise and softly call, 'Good night and joy be with you all.'"

1 gallon apple cide	1 bottle red wine
¼ cup mulling spices	1 cup dark rum
3 additional cinnamon sticks	1 cup brandy
½ cup honey	pinch salt
1 flask honey whiskey	

This recipe works well in a slow-cooker or any method that can be left on a very low heat for a long time, and yields enough for a full wake or a small card party, depending upon individual tolerance.

Gently heat the cider, the wine, and the honey with the spices and additional cinnamon sticks. Taste the level of sweetness, and add a tiny pinch of salt if desired, more honey, or brown sugar to the party's requirements, and taste again. No more tasting until it's done, though, or there won't be any left. Leave this mixture to warm on the lowest heat possible or in a slow-cooker on low until deeply fragrant. Never allow it to boil or get too hot, or the alcohol will cook away. About an hour before you'd like to serve it, remove the spices and add the rum and brandy. When this is warmed through, place the pint or flask of honey whiskey on the table with the ladle and glasses for guests to add to their glass as desired. Please do not overindulge and never, ever drink and drive.

"Good night, and joy be with you all."

About The Author

Grace O'Malley is a poet, author, and mermaid from the Appalachian mountains. She is presently working on a recipe collection of funerary offerings from history and trying to finance a bakery, two (hopefully) unrelated projects. Updates and links can be found at octoberesque.carrd.com

Two Weeks Wasn't Enough: Compounded Grief and Neurodivergence

By Kit Caelsto

On Friday, October 19, 2018, sometime between the end of Young & the Restless and when I went to awaken her from her daily, afternoon nap, my mother died. The dispatcher on the phone made me do CPR on her cold, lifeless body for nearly an hour until the first responders arrived (We live about thirty miles from town.) and they took over. After a few moments, when their faces said there was no hope, I asked them to stop. I knew my mother was gone. She'd went to sleep and never awakened, and as a nurse's daughter, I knew even if by some miracle I, or the first responders, revived her, she'd been without oxygen for too long. My mother would never return, and though I couldn't lay my hands on the paperwork at the time, I assured them she'd made her final wishes well known to me and others. She wanted a Do Not Resuscitate order. We'd talked about that quite often, including during her final stay in the hospital. The first responders agreed, and my mother was pronounced dead. My role as her caretaker was done. I could go on and live my life, right? Couldn't it? Wasn't that how this was supposed to go?

I'd been her full-time caretaker, our roles reversing so that it was I who took care of her personal needs, all of her needs after the nursing home discharged her against medical advice because they had a private pay patient lined up for her room. That they'd done no physical therapy didn't matter to the doctors who wanted to know why she wasn't up and walking and why her strength didn't miraculously return after three months in the local rehabilitation center. They didn't believe me when I'd said that against doctor's orders, no physical therapy had been done. The occupational therapist reviewed the notes, agreed with us that the nursing home had really neglected their duty, but none of that mattered anymore. My mother was dead. I no longer had to fight and advocate to get her something more than the basic care the local doctors grudgingly provided. And living in a small town there was no attorney to take a malpractice case, certainly not against the "best" nursing home in town. The state complaints had gone nowhere. The complaints to the Medicare people had gone nowhere either. We had been abandoned, and it'd be an eerie counterpoint to what would happen to me later.

Her cause of death was listed as her congestive heart failure stemming from the endocarditis she'd been diagnosed with in 1999. Add in being a diabetic who until I'd finally convinced her to allow me to help somewhere around 2005, had been unable to afford her medicine, and the cards had been stacked against her for a while. The cause of death was clear to the officials, and none of it reflected her lived experience from January 2017-October 2018, or the way we'd had to fight to get the very basics of her care done. Back in 1999, she'd never been expected to live long enough to get out of the hospital, let alone, nearly twenty years more. At least she was no longer in pain, people said. And I tended to believe it. Mom hated not being able to walk, to go out and see her horse. She'd been reliant upon a wheelchair and hoyer lift for mobility for nineteen months. One month for each year we'd gotten with her now that I think about it.

On the Monday morning after her Friday death, I'd called my employer. I was told that I could have two weeks off bereavement and then I'd need to return to the office. I'd been working from home since her fall to be her full-time caretaker. I thought that was a generous policy, appreciated their consideration, and then, the first full week in November, I returned to the office. After all, when my father had died in the middle oo's of cancer, I'd been given three days by the big bank.

It was only once I returned to the office that my nightly PTSD nightmares (mostly work related) began anew.

A year later, I was left with only one other coworker in the office as the business laid off half of its employees. About six months later, after the pandemic hit, we all went to work from home to be safe. We'd never come back to the office again, and in the end, two years after the staff was halved, employee numbers would half again, and I'd be left as the only employee. It took nearly three years after mom's death for all the grief I'd never processed, all the tears I'd never shed for either dad or mom to finally burst free, and I knew, deep in my heart, that two weeks not been enough time to grieve, but also, I'd never managed to grieve my father because I'd had to return to work back then, and I hadn't stopped working. I also realized that the summer of 2021 had been the start of severe autistic burnout. The two things—grief and autistic burnout—were inextricably linked.

Connecting The Dots Grief by Grief

I'd started having panic attacks after the staff was halved. I still remember the look on my boss' face when she asked why I'd been so scared when they'd asked me into the conference room to talk to me that afternoon. I reminded her that I had complex PTSD from my prior work for nearly sixteen years at a major bank. I'd been laid off in 2012 and that had prompted a 500 mile move to fulfill not just my dreams of living in the country, but also my mother's. My boss had smiled, laughed a little and said, "I thought you were over that. We're good employers." I now wonder if she was trying to convince herself more than me. Her words still haunt me because good employers wouldn't do what they did.

I said nothing, though. Don't make trouble. Don't get anyone mad at you. Those were the maxims that had been pounded into my brain by all those years of bullying and abuse. Stay down. Be a good worker. Get shit done. Don't cause problems. You'll be fine.

Except, I wasn't.

Christmas weekend 2019, I'd had my first panic attack, waking up in the middle of the night with horrible heartburn and a racing heart. But, just like the doctors had pretty much abandoned mom, there was no referrals made to a cardiologist. Just a prescription for some anxiety meds. That's all it was, right? That's all it had to be. With the medication, I was finally able to recognize my panic attacks; it was easy to do when you were having multiple ones a day from dealing with customers and coworkers and a boss who are all good friends with each other and leaving you out of every in-joke, every conversation. I vibrated with anxiety and tried to keep it wrapped deep inside, so no one knew. Don't make waves. Don't cause problems.

Losing mom had not just left a hole in my heart; it'd also reduced my income by 40%, so I needed the job. Living in a small town left me with few options. Fewer still when you figured that the lack of rural broadband meant no remote work. I was lucky my employer had tolerated my quirky country internet.

When I'd had my second full-blown, awake me in the wee hours of the morning with a 150bpm heart rate, panic attack a year later, I went to the behavioral healthcare clinic and they added a medicine to help with the physical symptoms, and when I explained what I'd gone through, were the ones to officially give me the diagnosis of chronic PTSD. It was my first experience with a self-diagnosis becoming official; and as someone who had been medically gaslit for years about my actually diagnosed fibromyalgia, the experience was a game changer. The diagnosis gave me something to hang onto. It gave me a new way of processing the world, and it opened the door to my grief.

It wasn't until the summer of 2022 when I'd come as close to a diagnosis of autism as I could locally. I didn't, and still don't, have the money for the official diagnosis from the local college a hundred miles away. But what I did have was a therapist who listened for a while and who did some research. She agreed. Yes, after 46 years, I finally had the truth. I wasn't broken or wrong, or even a failure, I was autistic.

And oh my god did everything make so much sense, though I had yet to know the depth of my grief.

You see, my mother had emotionally abused me, and this, combined with severe bullying in school, not to mention the hostile work environments, including my current one, in which I found myself, that combined to provide the basis for the cPTSD diagnosis. However, it wasn't until I realized I was autistic, that I received the confirmation, and connected with others in the #ActuallyAutistic community, that I realized so much about myself. I finally had the space after my mother's death, after a return to working from home so I wouldn't have to deal with the sensory hell that was working in an office (especially one painted bright shades of lime green and orange) and after not having to deal with a gaslighting coworker even remotely, that I finally found space to breathe. To process. And to realize the sheer weight of the grief which I'd been carrying around.

My dream had been to never return to the office at all. Someday I'd make enough money with my writing, with my business, that I'd just quit and do my own thing, taking care of my mother until she could stand and walk. We could do it—the two of us against the world. That's how it'd always had been. Except, her death meant it was just me against the world, and I was so alone, so ashamed by how little I'd accomplished, and how much I'd failed. I'd never meant to work a full-time job again after my layoff. I should have been able to be self-employed, to parlay my work into an income. I was making minimum wage at my day job (less than half the average wage in my industry due to small town and niche software), that I couldn't even reproduce that kind of income in self-employment chafed at me each and every day.

Failed at being self-employed. Failed at keeping my mother alive. (Never mind that we'd had nineteen years the medical experts weren't expecting us to have.) And the weight of all that grief crushed me.

More grief came. In October 2021 my aunt, the one who'd raised me like a mother, passed away after living with severe chronic illness for many years. There wasn't any bereavement leave for that. I counted myself lucky to get a "that's too bad" in the company chat room; I was the only employee by then and couldn't afford to attend the funeral anyway. In December 2021 we lost a dear pet cat to a sudden illness. And other "oh that's too bad", but no bereavement leave as others in the company had taken for the loss of their beloved pets. In August 2022, I lost the senior most horse of my herd. I didn't say anything by then. I knew my grief, my feelings, didn't matter anymore. At least not to them. The horse's age had been unknown;

she'd been a rescue. Although she'd just had a routine procedure, it was also quite possible her heart had simply given out. We'll never know. And frankly, by this time, I'm surprised mine hadn't done the same.

Each loss, each new layer of grief, I tamped down. Went on. That's what I was supposed to do; that's what I always did. So I went to work, my health getting worse and worse. The summer before my coworker left (Summer 2021), I swore I'd be self-employed. I'd quit this job and not look back before I had to return to college to seated classes in the fall. Except, that didn't happen.

Then my coworker left.

I'd make it then. Six months, tops. Sure. Only, I had no idea the weight of this grief, the weight of expectations, and the weight of everything.

I didn't know it, but I had toppled into autistic burnout.

And when my coworker left, leaving me to be the only employee, in spite of all the promises made that they wouldn't abandon me, that they wouldn't overwork me, that I'd get vacation. They lied.

They abandoned me. It's now been 13 months since my coworker left, and I have yet to be asked "you doing okay?" "do you have all the resources you need?". I'm writing this on the day before Thanksgiving, and it's the second year in a row they hadn't even bothered to say "Happy Thanksgiving".

I have worked 385 days as of today without a day off, weekends included. Thankfully not long on the weekends, but billable time nonetheless. That's okay, I'm not getting paid for overtime, and the fact that my boss couldn't even be bothered to provide a 2022 Company Holiday calendar meant I don't get holidays off either. That's okay. I didn't get Thanksgiving or Christmas off last year either once my coworker had left. Why am I telling you this? Because this is grief, too.

The grief of believing that I was liked. That these people considered me a friend, only to find out that they couldn't even be bothered to do the bare minimum as an employer. You don't treat friends this way, at least I don't think so. I'm autistic, remember? We don't do so well in the friend department. But I wouldn't treat a friend this way. (Don't worry. The company is small enough to slide right through state and federal loopholes against such behavior. This isn't illegal. Welcome to rural Missouri, USA, and I'm supposedly working for one of the "good" employers in town. I don't even want to try one of the others. Better the abandonment and abuse I know then trying to deal with it from someone new. Autistic people don't like change, remember?)

Grief piled upon grief, piled upon grief.

Small town, little employment prospects in my industry locally, lack of rural broadband...more grief.

My health getting worse, undergoing a medical procedure that was designed to resolve a long-term health issue only to figure out that no, this is part of my anxiety, part of my autism sensory processing issues, and it will probably never go away until I'm self-employed...more grief.

Losing not one, but two businesses under the weight of anxiety and burnout...still more grief.

Until I don't know what's me and what's grief. What's my personality and what's grief? And does it really matter anymore?

Grief is Like an Onion

I have no answers, so I do as I often do, and turn to analysis. If I can't feel my way out of a situation, something that's tough for an autistic individual to do at times, then I'll think my way out. And the analogy I've come up with is that grief is like an endless onion. Instead, we simply work on layer after layer. And if we're dealing with sensory overwhelm, trying to make it through each day, then we don't have the quiet and solitude we need to process each layer. So it just sits.

Sometimes we find that the grief layers itself up again, so when we think we're getting into the deeper layers, we discover we've still barely scratched the surface. A common grief meme talks about how the size of the grief inside us doesn't shrink. Instead, the container holding the grief—us—grows larger. I'm not sure this is true for neurodivergent individuals.

Don't get me wrong. We do grow and change. But it seems to me neurotypical people are able to shrink their grief, that eventually they grow their lives to encompass it, to make it seem less than it really is. As someone living with neurodivergence in the form of Autism and ADHD (not to mention the Generalized Anxiety Disorder and Major

Depressive Disorder diagnoses given pre-autism diagnosis), my grief ebbs and flows. Just as someone with ADHD can forget about something if they don't see it every day, they, or rather I, can forget about my grief. And then it's back, as fresh and raw, at the same layer, or maybe even closer to the surface, than it's been before, and I work through it again.

Grief has a habit of sneaking up on people, both neurotypical and neurodivergent. Hearing holiday carols in the store for the first time evokes tears and memories—both good and bad. As the wheel of the year turns, the late October-middle January timeframe is difficult for me due to losses. Sometimes the onion gets peeled a bit more after a good cry, then it sits there, hanging out, drying out, ready to be discovered anew.

I dream of being able to process my grief, to work through all the loss and the shame that goes along with that loss. No one talks to you about the shame. Grief and shame often go hand-in-hand. The grief is the processing of the loss. And if we don't process it within a timeframe that others, often neurotypicals, seem acceptable, then they are likely to shame us for that grief. So there's shame that comes from outside of us.

There's also the shame that comes from within. Bargaining is one of the stages of grieving. For many the bargaining is with God or some other deity. Others see the bargaining as being with themselves. They blame themselves for the loss, for the grief caused.

If only I'd been better at self-employment.

If only I hadn't been autistic and so bad at making and maintaining friendships. Maybe if I hadn't been my weird, oddball self my bosses wouldn't have abandoned me. It's my fault. That's why I work for low wages and even less appreciation. That's why I hadn't been able to save my mother. The shame spiral deepens. The same spiral gets tighter, faster, stronger, like a roller coaster hitting it's peak. Except it won't bring us safely back to a stop so we can disembark and go about our lives, having had the experience. Rather, it flings us out of the final loop to careen wildly through our life bouncing off the inevitable question, "what if?" "what if?"

Forgiveness Creates the Center of the Onion

Grief needs us to forgive ourselves. We cannot change the past. We cannot do anything different than we've already done, and what we've done is the best we could do in the moment.

So I forgive myself. I cannot change the past. All I can do is move forward, doing the best I can in any given moment.

Neurodivergent individuals need to forgive ourselves. I'd say everyone needs to forgive themselves in order to process their grief, but for us, it's more important. We have so many things that tell us that we're not good enough, not doing enough, not this enough, not that enough. When we stop listening to those "not enough"s and start forgiving ourselves, we create the center of the onion.

Instead of incessantly peeling layer after layer, we finally reach...the center. Forgiveness. And more importantly the belief that we deserve forgiveness, permission to forgive ourselves. Psychologists might tell you that you must forgive the person who wronged you. However, I find solace in Deborah Schurman-Kauflin Ph.D.'s words, "If you find yourself in this quandary, remember that only you can make this decision. This is one area where you have control. With time you may find it in your heart to forgive, or you may not. As you work through your healing process you find the things that bring peace and light into your life. How you feel is how you feel, and no one can dictate that to you no matter how hard he or she tries. Your heart is your own. Your spirit is your own. Your growth is your own.". (https://www.psychologytoday.com/us/blog/disturbed/201 208/why-you-dont-always-have-forgive)

The control you have is over yourself. And even if hindsight provides clarity on things you could have done differently, as it does for all of us, know that you did the best you could with the information you had in that moment. If you can, forgive yourself. That, to me, is the best thing any of us, but especially neurodivergent people can do to process grief.

Even if you can't forgive yourself, because there's no shame in being in that place, I think it's important to at least contemplate the possibility of forgiving yourself. To me, the forgiveness is what helps you to grow, to expand larger than the grief within. And that is the lesson, even as I'm still working through this grief, that I've finally arrived at, more than four years past my mother's death. Two weeks is not enough. Whatever time the business gives you off work for grief is not enough. Processing grief takes so much more than three days or two weeks. It takes time, space, being able to turn down the sensory overload, and a little bit of forgiveness.

I have no magic answer to my own grief. I have no answer to fix any of the issues. But the one thing I can do, is I can forgive myself. And that feels like a good starting point.

After living 46 years without an autism diagnosis, Kit Caelsto is finally figuring out who they are and who they want to be. They're a fat, agender, neurodivergent, disabled farmer yogi living in the Missouri Ozarks with their spouse, a sacred herd of horses, enough cats to be misgendered as a "crazy cat lady", a flock of beloved poultry including SuperDuck, the house duck, and Lugh, the house rooster. They're passionate about helping those who don't fit into society's boxes find creativity and wellness, and have been a published author for over two decades writing fiction and nonfiction.

They believe in autistic liberation, disability justice, fat acceptance, and radical, amazing self-love.

Website: https://chickenyogi.com; https://eponaauthorsolutions.com; https://unscramblet.com; https://kitauthor.com (which may still be a work in progress at the time of publication)

Looking Back: Grieving the Mask
By Jay Graves

Introduction

Throughout the majority of my life, I have felt as though I didn't belong anywhere that I wound up. Things I was supposed to understand, I didn't, and things I wasn't supposed to know anything about were hidden special interests for me. However, I did my best to conform and build a life that would typically be considered comfortable, successful, and above all would appear "normal." At the beginning of my educational journey into neurodiversity, I had put myself and everyone I was responsible for into a typical nice home with a fence and a yard in a good neighborhood. I had a good job and maintained everything to make sure I appeared typical to anyone who might observe from the outside. This life was built for a typical person but, though I tried, I have never been typical and appearing so meant that I was perpetually living for a carefully constructed mask, not myself.

The life I had built was not motivated by my understanding of the world, but the fear of consequence and, as a result, was not in my best interests as a person. I wasn't yet aware that I was neurodivergent at the time of my burnout. In fact, I had absolutely no idea what that meant or how it had influenced my entire life, in particular how it affected my mental health living in the world around me. Discovering and accepting my neurodivergence meant that I had to leave the mask of typicality behind and lose the life that was built for it. Losing an entire life and the access it afforded me was suffocating and tragic even if that life was ultimately unhealthy and never truly meant for me. There was extreme grief in the essential loss of an entire life. However, the lessons which were learned in surviving the loss of that life gave way to a new birth that turned out to be the only way for me to keep living.

Forming the Mask

The person that I was before my burnout was someone other than me. From infancy to very recent adulthood, every decision that I made in the calculus of who I had become to that point was nothing more than the result of a lifetime of forceful conditioning. Because of the way that my brain processes information and interacts with the external world I was never allowed the opportunity to understand the topics I was being taught. The rigid standards of neurotypical social interactions were not applicable to or effective in teaching me a variety of subjects and therefore the way that I learned most things was through a fear of punishment. There was no understanding or allowance for proper processing, just an ultimatum for nearly every decision. I was never taught any real motivation other than to avoid abuse which resulted in the formation of a mask. A life built for a person other than myself.

During my crucial developmental early childhood years, the conditioning came primarily from isolation and punishment conditioning informed by religious fundamentalism and typical mainstream culture. Corporeal punishment was the standard acceptable method of conditioning for parents to teach their children lessons when understanding failed, and the bullying kicked in when parents weren't there to do it. Self-discovery was heavily restricted and conformity was conditioned through punishment in every situation. Fear, paranoia, and the proclivity to accept abuse as a learning method became a significant personality trait and formed the foundations of the mask.

Through adolescence the conditioning was more institutionalized and subtle. As the influence of the church and my parents began to fade, the rigid standards and cultural hegemony of public schooling had already been going strong and took over the role of conditioning compliance in true systemic fashion. I brought my fear and proclivity to accept abuse with me into school and, looking back, it was very obvious how it influenced everything I did. I didn't understand homework or why it was so difficult for me to get started or finish it. I struggled with disabilities over reading from print on paper and just conceded defeat in every instance, considering myself a failure and asking for help typically resulted in frustration. I was diagnosed at the request of the school as ADHD early on which merely became a justification for more intense conditioning and social isolation.

A good portion of my time outside of school was spent isolated in one way or another as a result of punishment for my scholastic performance. I began to stand up for myself in school at one point and remember being told "We don't want you knowing how to fight" when I inquired about taking self-defense. Soon after, I found myself in an inpatient teen crisis unit because the people I was living with at the time claimed to be afraid of me, but it was punitive. I was disallowed the ability to drive when I was old enough because I "couldn't be trusted" with the responsibility. Looking back this was all purely a result of discrimination against my disabilities, but I was a child and figured I was just rotten.

"The world needs ditch-diggers" an adult once told me, and that's what they were sure to condition me to be. No amount of punishment seemed to make it easier for me to complete schoolwork nor did it make reading on paper easier. I was a problem child and a troubled teen according to everyone I encountered. School wasn't for me, and I was unstable enough to be feared for some reason. I didn't really understand any of it, but I really wanted to avoid the abuse of being my honest self. So, I put my head down and avoided standing up for myself through the rest of school. I spent a lot of time outside of school doing work for other people or being scolded for unfinished homework. My senior year of high school was spent working a full-time job as a part of the work-study program. As soon as I could, I took my 1250 SAT scores and 1.9 GPA then set out to be a ditch-digger of some sort.

Maintaining the Mask

After just barely graduating high school, I attempted to live on my own and continued to work for a few years, still never quite fitting in. I was being regularly passed over for advancement at any job that I wound up at even when I believed I was the most qualified. I had no access to support of any kind past random strangers which didn't always turn out well in itself. I didn't understand why I was on my own and nobody would help, but I attributed it to me just being a failure and misunderstanding the rules again. I couldn't afford to live on my own and had been kicked out of every home I had been in so far. Since I was disallowed from getting my driver's license when I was originally old enough, nobody ever taught me how to drive. My suspended license and unaffordable insurance was evidence of this, and I found myself in a desperate situation with no way to get around, no support, and ultimately unable to afford to live on my own.

I wound up joining the military and specifically volunteering for a frontline combat position. I promoted it to myself and others as some spontaneous honorable act of patriotism but, looking back, it was primarily to avoid homelessness or die if I failed. Housing was provided and the regimentation of daily life in the military seemed to work well for me. On top of solving the housing issue, what I viewed as some of my special skills were applicable to what

I was doing as a grunt Marine. After all, I could dig ditches pretty well. I still didn't feel like I belonged, but I didn't have a choice and neither did any of my peers, so I mostly fit in. More importantly, I finally seemed to fit the model of what I was conditioned to believe an acceptable person was. I believed that I had finally built that acceptable person and possibly even a mask that people seemed to be impressed by.

After all the military training, getting married, and two combat deployments, I seemed to finally fit in and had the opportunity to go to school as a result. I went into college with the intention of becoming a finance major and left as a Philosopher of Cognitive Science with a double minor, neither of which were in finance. My major had become philosophy with a concentration in the philosophy of the human mind accompanied by a double minor in cognitive science and psychology. The phenomena of human consciousness had become my special interest and seemed to draw me into the field on its own. I could work on a computer screen and understand the material; I was fascinated with the subject matter and absorbed everything. School was very different on my own than it was when everyone was forcing me to learn their way.

The material in the psychology minor courses that I was exposed to dealt very heavily with the basics of behaviorism, specifically with conditioning and learning. It also included a course named "Abnormal Psychology" that interested me particularly. It was weird stuff and I liked weird things. That course contained a lot of interesting information regarding pathological psychological disorders along with an overview of Autism Spectrum Disorder. I found myself checking off the criteria in a self-diagnosis fashion and, at the time, I rationalized it away as foolishness and a possible psychosomatic type of response to the material. I did well with my focus material, found a special interest and enjoyed school somehow.

Looking back this was when my first adult burnout began. After a failed marriage, three DUIs and exhausting the funding for school just before I was able to graduate it should have become clear that the mask was no longer working for me. I couldn't handle my remaining elective course load and no longer qualified for affordable housing on campus as a result of my divorce. So, I had to leave school without finishing. After this failure I again found myself in a desperate housing situation, and my license was about to be revoked. I had to find a place to live before my lease on campus ran out and hopefully find a way to keep my license. I had no support structure available and could not afford to live anywhere near walkable living. I found a garage on the other side of the country in which I could afford to live and keep my car. So, that's what I did and where I went.

I continued to work at building the life that I believed I was supposed to. I began a serious relationship, took on the responsibility of raising two young children and had put myself and that family into a nice home with a fence and a yard in a nice neighborhood. I had a good job as my primary source of income and was working 50-60 hour weeks to support it all. It seemed like everything was working according to everything the mask was supposed to look like, and I was no longer living in a garage like a failure.

Autistic Burnout

There was a distinct cyclic pattern to living with the mask always on, and again I found myself in a deep depression. Anxiety was constant and only interrupted by the blur of commuting and working for ten or more hours a day. I had been saddled with nearly the full financial burden of the family as my partner found herself in a deep battle with a very costly substance abuse problem. She maintained secrecy over it until it was obviously out of control and all that I knew in the meantime was that I had somehow effectively become a single parent who was gone for 10-15 hours a day, alone to care for two children most nights, and broke now as well. I began to have problems with insomnia and started using alcohol to self-medicate as I had done in the past when the mask wasn't working.

I began to recognize that every decision I was making had been entirely informed by the conditioning and trauma of my past to avoid abuse until it was unavoidable. This wasn't my stuff, these weren't my friends, this wasn't my job or my home, and this wasn't my life. I didn't know who this person was that I built all these things for, but it was not me. My past to that point was rooted in supporting others without regard for my own personal well-being in order to maintain the outward appearance of what I was conditioned to believe was normal. I was now able to identify the abuse in multiple major relationships and I began to address it as such.

I addressed the abuse in my relationship. I was caring for two children for a now mostly absent mother as well as working full-time. In addressing the abuse and its effects, a significant substance abuse issue was revealed, and the reasoning for things began to make more sense. While the issues caused by her struggle with substance abuse weren't deliberately to harm me, my conditioned proclivity to accept abuse as normal clouded my judgment and prioritized the outward mask for my inner health. I stuck around and bore the burden of the entire relationship just to avoid her anger or discomfort. This abuse quickly turned out to be the only basis for the relationship to continue and so it ended. The family I had built for the mask was gone, along with the two children I had been raising. Due to the financial drain of recent events, I had already found myself back in a small apartment and the house with the yard was already gone.

I addressed the abuse in my employment. I was working 50-60 hours a week at a job that paid a daily rate and hired me under the pretense of 8-hour days. The 8-hour days and jobs quickly turned into 10-12 hours bookmarked by an hour commute each way for the same daily rate. I began to notice that the further and longer solo jobs were almost exclusively assigned to me. When I confronted my boss asking for a raise with the extra work, I wound up getting a $40 gas card per week instead. I was fortunate to complete a day of jobs earlier than 8 hours on one instance and left to go home. My employer had seen me from his vacation on a security camera turning my vehicle in that day earlier than 4pm and confronted me about it. He threatened to take that day's pay. I put the gas card on the counter and left forever. My tolerance for abuse had faded completely.

Gradually the mask eroded until it was gone entirely along with the life built to support it. Without my willingness to accept abuse as normal living circumstances, my relationships with others at that time had no healthy foundation and crumbled immediately. While I believed that I had addressed my problems in a healthy way with my health finally being a consideration, any opportunity to progress in the life which I had built to that point was unrecoverably gone. I was burned out, again, from maintaining the mask for three decades and I was alone, unemployed, in a strange place, and everything was gone.

With no guidance or support there was only depression and anxiety now...again. Not only was everything gone, it was unrecoverably gone and I really didn't want to believe it. I had no idea how I was going to afford to live, where I could go, or what I could do otherwise. This started a period of depression the depths of which I didn't think possible. There were no positive emotions, smiles were just remnants of the mask and only seen in public. The fake happiness which I had previously ridden to success before was now only applicable for very brief periods of time spent during impersonal chores and tasks. My life had become saturated with grief.

Grieving the Mask

About two weeks before I quit my job I remember saying "They're just going to tell me I'm autistic and throw drugs at me." to my co-worker while I went through the process of being re-evaluated for VA disability. My time in the psychology courses revealed to me the possibility that I may be autistic long before this. However, as is still too common in academia, I was educated on autism only as a diagnosable "disorder." Now, as I understood it, not only was I a failure based on everything I had been conditioned to believe, but I was possibly an autistic failure as well. My psychology was 'abnormal'. I couldn't hide it any longer, and everything that I had worked so hard to achieve that may have once covered this fact up was gone. I really didn't see a way things could get better, and now I was not only a failure, but an autistic failure. Great...

I had been self-medicating with alcohol to combat my insomnia for some time at this point. I had recently fooled myself into believing that I could use it medicinally to fall asleep at night. It quickly evolved into day long binges just to induce amnesia for another day. There was no medicating my way out of this. As far as I had learned, my life was essentially over, and I treated myself accordingly. However, although I was alone and dealing with the systemic abuse that is poverty, at least I didn't have to suffer the abuse of maintaining the mask anymore.

The effects of conditioning on how I slept was becoming more apparent as my burnout continued. Between church, school, work, and military service I was never really allowed to sleep on my schedule. Now while grieving, it was all late nights spent awake going back and forth between trying to fix unfixable problems and maintaining some hope to hold on to neurotypical standards. Still denying my disability, I took a job and began working again to meet financial obligations. On the third night of working, I was pulled over on my commute home for speeding and wound up in jail for my behavior. I was grieving the loss of my mask...poorly.

I was about to learn that this was the beginning of my first recognized adult autistic burnout. Moreso it was the most recent one at the end of a series of unrecognized ones. I suspected myself to be autistic since first encountering the diagnostic criteria for it in college. I began seeking out further information on autism and discovered more modern research into it as a social disability and more broadly, I discovered the field of neurodiversity.

There was no mention in the psychology minor of the social model of disability and how it applies to any sort of neurodivergence or any other applicable disability. The social model of disability acknowledges the existence of socially constructed barriers to people with disabilities that prevent them from achieving their full independence whereas, the medical model ascribes a pathological disorder to the individual's natural resistance to conform with accepted subjective normative social standards. Nothing in my psychology courses covered the possibility that the behavioral traits associated with any type of neurodivergence could be the effects of systemic barriers or conditioning. They didn't even acknowledge neurodiversity as a concept.

I was officially diagnosed as ADHD early on at the school's request, confirmed it on my own, and was now comfortable calling myself autistic as well. I continued to explore spaces related to my own neurodivergence and found loose-knit communities of a variety of neurodivergent people discussing their experiences in the context of social barriers and misunderstanding-based conditioning. I was definitely not alone, and the causes for suffering were all rooted in the same type of prejudice. Too many things made sense in shared autistic and ADHD experiences when examined through the lens of neurodiversity. The prejudice of neurotypicality throughout my life became clear, and I began to be able to identify its influence at every perceived failure. I quickly learned to recognize the social barriers and uninformed conditioning responsible for the mask's very existence.

I am disabled, and it was time to finally admit that. I am autistic. I am ADHD. I am neurodivergent, and none of this meant I was ever a disordered version of some nebulous "normal." I had moved past my formal education into recognizing my own neurodivergent experience as well as the commonalities of my experience to others in the neurodivergent community. My disabilities were never recognized as a lack of support before now, and I swallowed the lie that I was broken instead. The way my brain processes information is significantly different than any mechanism of learning I was exposed to up until this point past forceful compliance conditioning. I was not disabled because a part of me was broken. The way everyone treated me in teaching me was very broken and this disabled me.

Looking back on things while grieving I began to recognize more and more of the institutionalized and systemic barriers to my neurotype involved in my "failures" along with the hegemonic bullying and prejudice against neurodivergence at the center of it all. Autistic people are not a broken version of non-autistic people to be corrected and better made to conform. In the same way, ADHD people are not disordered versions of non-ADHD people. Both autistic and ADHD people are disabled by outdated social standards primarily in the conditioning and learning process. Neurodivergent people can only be effectively accommodated, we cannot be cured or conditioned into normality. My lifetime of cyclic burnouts was simply evidence of society's failure to properly support a multiply neurodivergent person and not a failure of mine.

My educational journey into neurodiversity and connecting with the neurodivergent community gave me perspective. I was not a failure; I was failed by the structures around me like so many neurodivergent others. The behavioral constraints and hidden social rules of neuro-conformity and mainstream culture did not promote healthy mental states or habits for my unique neurotype. I was disabled by the world around me and its inability to properly accommodate my very way of thinking.

This new perspective allowed me to cope with the grief of losing a life that was never truly mine anyway. I accepted my disability and mental health became the priority in my life. I was determined to use what I had learned about myself to fix what neuro-conformity had conditioned into my brain and body. Living under the mask was toxic to me simply due to how my brain functioned to process the external world regardless of how well I fit the typical model outwardly. I only ever attempted to conform to social norms as a means to avoid abusive punishments, not because I understood them or that they appealed to me. Losing the toxicity of a life informed entirely by abuse was an undeniably positive change and with this new perspective, the grief seemed misplaced. I grieve the time lost, the suffering endured, and the effort spent but can no longer bring myself to grieve for the life that I lost.

Looking forward, I realize that I am not disordered; the social structures around me are disordered for me. Current status quo conformity isn't healthy for me. While that may not necessarily change current access to support or accommodations, it is significant for me to understand that I am not a broken typical and can move forward with that knowledge. It is an opportunity for a new start and to build a life informed by who I actually am. Education into who I actually am turned out to be the ultimate coping mechanism for the grief of having lost my mask. Now I understand that I have the opportunity to build a life for me and by me. Regardless of what transpires in the future, it will be honest and informed by my choices and natural tendencies.

I lost everything and found myself. I know who I am, and I am neurodivergent.

Neurodiversity is a natural and beautiful part of the human experience.

Neurodivergence is not a disorder and 'disability' is not a dirty word.

We are disabled by our access to support.

Your burnouts are not your fault.

You are not your mask.

I believe in you.

About The Author

Jay Graves is a multiply neurodivergent autistic and ADHD Philosopher of Cognitive Science educated at Rutgers University as well as a multiple tour USMC combat veteran.

Grieving Loss of Friendships: How I Experience Friendship Loss, and How I Ultimately Deal With It

By Joseph Eric Gitau

I've always struggled making friends. It's not that I don't like people; it's more so that people intimidate me. So when someone wanted to be friends with me, it always sets of a chain reaction of RSD (Rejection Sensitive Dysphoria) in me because I'm still at the point where I feel like I must have to offer something to the other person for them to actually like me. And because of that I always struggle to create meaningful bonds, because I either pretend to be someone I'm not, or be myself and risk people getting weirded out.

Ironically enough, it was me pretending to be someone I'm not that caused me to lose the most friendships. The more I accepted my ADHD and Bipolar diagnoses, the less I ended up 'masking'. And people who knew me while I was 'masking' weren't able to get used to the new me. So I did lose a lot of friends because of that. But there were others who just went quiet. And those were the friendships that hurt me the most. The ones where I didn't know why they weren't talking to me anymore. Those send me into a spiral of questioning whether I was good enough, and looking over every interaction with intense scrutiny looking for any mistake I could have made that would make people not like me anymore.

And that's the thing, I didn't realize that it didn't take much for people to drift apart. It wasn't a question of whether I was too much, whether they accepted me for who I was. It was more a question of was that they were at a point in their life where they needed someone different in their life. They didn't hate me. I didn't know that these two could be exclusive. No one told me that. I ended up having to figure it out on my own since it was one of those silent rules that we're expected to know. It sucks that we often have to figure these things on our own, because we're often told that we need to stop using ADHD as an excuse.

But it gets even worse. What happens when you know that because of your struggles, that someone runs out of patience and decides that you're not trying hard enough? That you're hiding behind your ADHD to get out of taking accountability? Those hurt because it always feels like your struggles are not being taken seriously. While losing people because they can't accept the new you can be tough, knowing that someone you thought would always be there has hit a limit to how much they can tolerate you is somehow even worse. And when you're someone like me who struggles to voice their needs and concerns, it can often blow up in your face. Especially when you constantly take on more than you can handle out of fear that anything less will make people dislike you.

How I ended up dealing with it was by bottling up all my needs, as unhealthy as that sounds. My thought process was 'if I can keep them happy, then they have no reason to leave me'. Thus I gave up my own happiness to make others happy. Never sticking out more than was necessary was basically my motto. And because of this, I never could trust myself to nurture bonds beyond the friendship stage, even if I wanted to. If I couldn't keep a friend happy, how could I even begin to even try to keep a potential partner happy? It couldn't, no, wouldn't work.

So as friends went quiet, or just lost contact, I ended up sitting in my corner, confused and mad at myself. I would try to reach out to them from time to time, but then the silence would happen again.   Not knowing what happens sends me into a spiral of RSD that often takes a while to get out off. And one of the best ways I've come up to deal with it is writing. A lot of my stories are based on how I wish a lot of these friendships went. You could say I have a lot of regrets about how things went. And knowing that I might not have an opportunity to change things, or make things right, I needed a way to let go of the regrets. And therapy has been too expensive for me to use that as a viable option, as much as I would have loved to go.

Despite all the regrets I've had over the years when it comes to friendships, I really can't bring myself to hate them. A lot of these friends have given me great memories, despite the fact that I can seem needy and emotional. I know that everything I've experienced in the past doesn't mean that they're a part of those bad memories. Yet, I know that somehow, I lack the experience, or even tack, to nurture long term friendships, or even relationships. But ultimately, I know that despite everything, I've come to learn that not everything is forever. Everything has a time, as blind as I am to the concept of time. I know a lot of my experiences aren't necessarily ND (neurodivergence) related. I mean, people do grieve over lost friends after all. I think that a lot of why I tend to lose friends is due to the fact that myself and those around me don't fully understand ADHD, Bipolar and how it affects how I interact with others.

Friends come and go, but yet, I've never understood why that was. To me, every lost friend was a judgment of my character. As I grew and accepted my diagnosis, I had to accept the fact that not everyone would stick around. I needed to figure out who I was, and what I wanted before I could ask anyone who would want to be friends with me to do walk this journey with me. This is my story in a sense.

About the Author

A writer, singer, blogger and content creator who just happens to have ADHD and Bipolar I. My current passion is creating expansive worlds and talking about the mental health issues that I've been facing. My work may not necessarily be J.R.R Tolkien worthy, or even be Shakespeare quality, but it is my own and that's important

Website: <u>Pillar.io/jgasparmiswired</u>

Compost
By Emma Barnes

How do we quantify grief?

Our pet, when gone, burns inside our bodies. We tickled them and the curl of their pelt tickled us right back. We rolled in the grass with them and vocalised our joy. They sang back. Their song played inside our bodies and back to them, to and fro, a call and return through our ears and our larynx. It is not metaphorical to say our loved ones "are a part of us". They roll in the grass of our nervous systems. Seven trillion tiny blades of grass - our nerves - ache for their touch when they are gone. Each blade embedded in soma, in tissues, and reaching at their proximal tips for a sun that has set. Where once these conduits gave and received life, without it they must find a new source. Like grass in an eternal night, they compost.

Compost needs heft and heat. A small pile rots cold and sours. But with heft it tempts critters known as *thermophiles* who come in their millions to chew and baste, turning a graveyard into a festival. With enough magicians the festival reaches a critical temperature (45°C) whereupon they reproduce. Minaturised life-and-death cycles, fractals in the spiritual realm, churn the pile and ready it to sustain the forms that reach up and out for the shining sun. If the living pile has too much material to work with - too much dead matter and too much oxygen, it will heat beyond its threshold (75°C), and either die quietly or combust in burning overwhelm.

This is what happens in our bodies when loves depart. Our nerves sing out for life's energy and don't hear back. Their roots break in numbers and make a heap inside us. At the right temperature, a little hotter than our blood, decomposition begins. Thermophiles gather and heat us up. We reach a point, a little hotter than usual, where compost grows inside us, transforming our lost past into humus for our future. Just like compost, we must sit in the perfect range lest the pile rots and sours (too cold) or burns us up on the inside (too hot). We measure grief with a thermometer.

I was too cold for the first 44 years, sour and confused. And then, with only three discoveries, I was burning beyond decay. Death? No, there was none of that. That's the thing about taking off a mask—people who loved the mask cannot stay. They glitch. And then they leave.

45°C

I had this love from the start. My sibling warned me that it was not safe for a stimming Autistic in the world we inherited. They supplied one-word invectives popular in the late 1970's but unutterable in 2022. I mutated from cute infant to transgressive toddler, and they sent the message clearly. I learned to tighten up. Forty odd years later, with their ableist disgust still intact, I loosened up and spoke clearly; "If you will not begin healing, I will not be in your life." They backed out of the room. This was my first taste of grief. Still held safe by a matrix of fictitious safety, my nerves decomposed in a small, gently heated packets. Within six months the remains of our connection was a rich humus in my body again.

50°C

An undiagnosed Autist himself, a psychiatrist, and an avid gardener, he brought his wounds from the 20th century, where the everyday violence of supremacy—race, gender, and ability—was barely labeled. He reproduced it in gentle ways, skirting detection and self-awareness. Notions of repair, and the accountability that repair demands, were anaethemic to his positionality—patriarchal and projective. Moreover, how could he understand that he may have misstepped? He had, after all, overcome the dictates of the catholic church by embracing a more progressive god— science and rationalism. He did not understand the language of boundaries, so I attempted for several years to engage him in the intellectual arena where he felt safe. We talked about his intellectual heroes, and I gently prodded at the edges of his psychiatric worldview. He was stiff and defensive. He could not bend a little to see my divergent being—trans and Autistic—from anywhere but in the pathologising prison where he had safely locked himself. He had his reasons. He played with my body when I was tiny and built a fortress around his shame—pathologising me from a young age; *unreliable, phantastic, pathological.* He first sent me to a colleague at 15 and next at 25. When the truth threatened to erupt, he told me I was "depressed" and prescribed me SSRIs. Twenty anaesthetised years later I tapered off and found my past still roiling underneath it all.

Saying goodbye to him was easy and now the heap inside metabolised the loss. It was easy because I was still safely privileged by gender and neuronormativity, having not come out of either closet.

60°C

Undiagnosed ADHD, a psychotherapist of analytic persuasion, fond of the silverware. She wore her mask more tightly than I did mine. Unpicking its fasteners in conversation with her proved intolerable for us both. She endured three quarters of a century supplicant to neuronormativity, to whiteness, to the patriarchy, and to money. In a safe enough room, she'd have noted the patriarchy's impact on her but none of the rest. We tussled with repair for a bit, but the looming truth was too much. She was getting close to 45°C herself, where the first thermophilic critters get busy. For my part, I was out of the gender closet and throwing the clippings of my privilege atop a pile that was hot enough already.

75°C

During two years of transition, my housemate and best friend held me steady and I, her. She was there when I noticed I wasn't a boy. She gently corrected my naive missteps toward femininity. She took me into her arms when my girlfriend revealed herself as a TERF, when my family turned on me, and when friend after friend became a ghost. I was her shoulder for equally wrenching ordeals. Support was unconditional and there was no part of our lives we didn't share, or so I believed. One day, sitting in our house, our material shell, I received her email. It announced her departure. To where it did not say. Why it did not say. Dust.

I can't be sure that the pile heated up then. I was numb throughout. My nervous system collapsed. I couldn't tie my laces, cook my food, let alone arrange the house move. Two friends came to my rescue. I sat lumpen while they boxed and cleaned. I had not been helped like that before. I had never asked.

For the hundred days that followed I pretended to be able to look after myself. I even tried to look after someone else and two dogs. It was hopeless. I asked the someone else to move elsewhere, and I found new homes for the dogs. I checked into the psych ward.

Over the following ten months the burning decomposition inside me spread outwards towards my skin and engulfed me. I was scorched earth.

80°C

In literary terms, losing a loved one can become an essay, or a meaningful book. Losing two, or three, or four, is too much for literary fiction. It's too thick. Too hot. It finds another genre; action or horror. Or if told straight it risks becoming "trauma porn". What kind of work, then, do you produce when you lose everyone, including yourself? Something unreadable, I suppose. Compost.

My losses were no longer regenerating with thermophiles. They had combusted. Instead of feeling emotions as a pressure here and a tingling there, there was heat all over, all day, every day. I had combusted. These were burning embers.

In the smoke of my charred nervous forest, I noticed something as hard to believe as the notion that I wasn't a man. I noticed I had never had a relationship. With anyone. Each connection between me and other humans was between my mask and another's ego. I didn't know them, and they didn't know me. What do you grieve if you've never known anyone, and nobody has ever known you?

I pondered what kind of people love a masked ego-pleaser. Those are the people I had drawn closest to me. My entire social world, composting inside me, was made of falsehoods. And that was only the superficial conundrum.

Beyond grieving every single relationship I never had but had believed in, I had next to acknowledge that every practice I had developed, each dream, each success and failure, was for someone else - for the mask. I did not exist. I never had.

I can take my lead from the Australian bush now. The banksia's rugged seeds are imprisoned by their parent in lignin. Only the heat of our periodic bushfires is intense enough to crack them open. When this happens, the younglings find themselves in the sun for the first time, amongst the burning remains of a forest. To us, that landscape speaks of tragedy, wounded animals and lost habitats. To a banksia seed, however, there is opportunity—first light. The seed will poke into the cinders and up into the air, structureless but for its instincts. Downwards, rooting to the earth, upwards into the sky, and outwards to touch its new siblings.

About the Author

Emma Barnes is a queer writer and bridge teacher living on Dharug Country in Sydney, Australia. She writes about the history of science, psychiatry, neurodiversity and healing, gender, and mad liberation. Her memoir is due at the publishers in June 2023. You can read her work at https://eggybing.medium.com/

Learning to Grieve
By Rory Bristol

As a nonbinary queer person from the American South, I learned two rules very early on: Emotions are not acceptable except for anger and celebration, and we *never* discuss sad things. These two neurotypical rules would clash with my autistic mind constantly for decades. From a young age, I learned to dissociate from my emotional responses in order to fit in. After all, if I don't feel my emotions, I can't show my emotions. Which is followed by another maxim: If I don't show my emotions, I won't be judged and excluded.

I had no idea how fundamentally this would shape my world view for the first 30 years of my life.

Of particular personal interest has been my relationship with grief. Grief has always been something unsafe, unseen, unheard, and unspoken. Any time death came up, even at church (you know, the place with all the answers about what happens when we die), a simple platitude of "they're in a better place" would be tossed out while most people looked uncomfortable and changed the subject as soon as they could physically manage it. No one cried. No one raged. The silence that followed death in my youth was palpable.

In junior high, my best friend and football teammate was named John. He was the first person to practice "catch" with me, and never mocked my fumbles and less-than impressive passes. His father would take us both out to dinner at truckstop restaurants that made me think fondly of my grandfather who was a trucker but lived far away. Some of my favorite childhood memories were just spending time with those two, knowing that they never judged me for a second.

One day, I arrived at school late, and when I was checking in with the school, a classmate named David came in the office. He had obviously been crying and was still sniffling. I asked him what was wrong, and he gave me a bewildered look. "John's dead." I turned to the secretary behind the desk. She said in a calm, quiet voice. "The principal announced it a few minutes ago over the intercom." I just stared at her, feeling like I was stuck on a loading screen. After a pause that lasted much too long, she asked David, "Do you need to call your mother?" He did. He left school because he knew he would be a mess if he stayed.

The secretary turned to me and asked, "Was John a friend of yours?"

I realized I was still staring. After a moment, though, I replied, "John is my only friend."

She coughed, that tiny polite cough Southern women do when you've said something obviously wrong or idiotic. "He **was** your only friend. But he's in a better place now." I knew I was supposed to say something, anything. I knew I was staring at her blankly but didn't know how to move forward from that moment. Eventually, she asked, "Do you need to call your parents?"

I shook my head, told her I was late, and needed to sign in. I went to class. I listened as the topics ranged from how John had died—shot while hunting without safety vests—to how John's friend David had **actually cried** in front of the whole class. He was one of the largest kids in our class, a farm kid, the picture of masculinity, and he had ***cried*** right there, in his seat. Fingers were pointed. Their mocking voices hushed when the teacher looked up but picked up again as soon as she was distracted. Before the end of the class, John's death wasn't the point of conversation anymore. By the end of the day, I'd heard the story of David crying in every class, but only heard conversation about John in that first class.

I still felt nothing. Not indignation that they were mocking a kid for his genuine and valid emotions, nor rage when the other kids said John deserved to die if he wasn't using safety equipment, and not when the teacher scolded the kids for making too much noise but ignoring the subject matter. All I had was numbness, a disconnection that would have driven me to distraction if I had been able to care about anything.

Over the coming years, that deep aching numbness would grow.

About two years later, my mother was waiting for us when we got home. She normally worked in the afternoon, which was why we took the bus. She said she had bad news. Then she broke down sobbing, completely unable to speak for several minutes. It was the most emotion I'd ever seen out of an adult in my life, and I was fourteen or so. Eventually, she choked out the words "Butch is dead," before falling over in a fit of inconsolable sobbing.

I had just learned that my paternal grandfather had died. I should have felt something, anything. But I didn't. But I couldn't stand the emptiness of staring into space. I moved into action. I told my youngest brothers that they could play video games after they finished their homework, but that I wouldn't actually check to make sure they had done it. My twin brother and I tag-teamed cooking dinner and consoling our distraught mother.

I had had no idea my mother had held Grandpa Butch in such esteem. They always seemed to needle each other over every possible point. She had split with my father when I was still a baby. Later, I learned that she had looked to Butch as a father figure since she was a teenager, and that that hadn't stopped with the dissolution of her relationship with my father. So, my mother needed consoling, and I was there to do it. So, I did. And I felt nothing.

Over the following days, I would despair at my lack of distress. I felt like grief should be cutting me like a barbed knife twisting in my guts. I felt like I shouldn't be able to go to school, or church, or anything else. But I did do those things. All the while, anger began to build up, like a demon demanding my attention every minute of the day. For months, I was constantly furious with everyone and everything.

Eventually, I came to recognize this anger as a complicated form of resentment. I was furious to learn that, unlike my friend John, Grandpa Butch hadn't died suddenly.

He had been terminally ill for years. When we visited my grandmother, there was obvious evidence that he had been in hospice for over a year, perhaps over two. There were pictures with newborns where he's wearing oxygen tubing and had bandages and bruises on his arms. Those newborns were preschoolers now. It had been a long, gradual decline for my grandfather, and not a single person in our massive family had ever thought to talk to the children about the reality that we would lose him, and that we couldn't know when that would be.

This anger terrified me. A couple of times, I lashed out and hurt people I cared about. This violated my own values, so I did the only thing I knew to do. I squashed that anger with everything I had. I continued to strive for the peace of detachment rather than the pain of being present. I had no sadness, and now I didn't even have anger. I never cried; I never felt regret or loss. I even stopped raging. Instead of feeling my emotions, I just continued existing in a forward direction until I stopped thinking about it.

My senior year in high school featured the most drawn-out death of my life. My close friend Elijah had muscular dystrophy and lived his entire high school existence knowing he could die any day. People born with MD often die in high school, with that risk climbing steadily beginning at age sixteen. Even twenty years ago, I was able to find enough information about his condition to know that he wasn't going to graduate. He had a severe case and was lucky enough to make it to our senior year.

We were friends for five years, following John's death. Those five years were transformative for me in ways I couldn't have expressed at the time. This was a war won on many fronts. The lessons I took from our friendship would alter my life in ways he'd never have been able to imagine.

First, I learned the value of living unapologetically as one is. Elijah had little time for other people's opinions, likely because he knew he had limited time and refused to give anyone his energy when it didn't serve him. He was obsessive with his interests and talked about them constantly. I learned almost everything I know about the Metroid video game universe from our conversations, despite playing it many times since. He could reproduce any art element he'd ever seen, carefully, slowly, and painfully drawn to scale, usually on the paper he was supposed to be doing schoolwork on. He would draw massively complicated vehicles, weapons, and armor from video games he loved, and never showed them off. He just did them for himself.

All of this flew in the face of our peers' mocking laughter, teachers' frustrated attempts to make him "focus on the important things," and constant nudging from his student aid. He focused on living a worthwhile life, and being true to himself, regardless of the feedback he received. He spent countless hours replicating the same 100+ video game designs from a game nobody else would admit they liked. He told people what he thought, if they asked, and didn't mince words. He didn't have many friends, but he cherished those of us who were close to him. I learned by watching. "This person, right here, is living unapologetically and being true to himself, even when it hurts."

This lesson would lead to me coming out as queer a few months after he passed and has continued to drive me toward celebrating my most authentic self. As I move through the world with a shopping list of labels, I learned to see the value that came from each of those labels. Whether it's my improved perspective with self-care that came from PTSD or my courage to stand and tell my truth that came from the validation I searched for and found in the queer community, I have learned to nurture the duality that comes with every facet of ourselves. There will always be challenges, but there will also always be joys—especially if you're being honest with yourself and about yourself.

Second, I learned the value of becoming comfortable with the idea of death. Elijah never talked about death directly. That was a specific taboo that seemed immutable. But Elijah did tell an awful lot of jokes—all of them funny, and many of them about his own inevitable death. After church, we would talk about the afterlife or what heaven could be like. He always said it doesn't matter what comes after. We are here, now, and what we're doing with that is what matters.

The memory of those conversations is still powerful and moving to me. These ideas that he introduced me to, mainly the idea of focusing on what we can know, do, and give to the world, planted seeds in my brain that would lead me into studying humans, in all our messy glory. I dedicated an unknowable amount of time learning about countless faith practices, theologies, philosophies, sciences, psychology, and physiology, all in my search to learn how to do better— be better—in the moment that is now.

This journey exposed me to the ever-growing "death positivity" movement, championed by content creators on

YouTube and other places on the internet that have frank, candid conversations about death. I learned about the different laws in America regarding the human corpse, and about other cultural approaches to handling the remains of a loved one. For the first time, I really began to feel like I knew how to grieve.

I was so, so wrong.

In 2011, my father died by suicide. He was drunk, he was ashamed, and he was desperate. It's not a great combination on the best of days, but it also happened to be the anniversary of Grandpa Butch's cremation, and his inability to talk about that grief, to manage it, and to move on from it, led him into a place he couldn't see the path out of. Some of my brothers had been playing in the street behind the car and had seen him headed for the car. Then they heard the shot and went to him. They found him bleeding out, but there was nothing they could have done. He was dead before emergency services could arrive.

They all lived with my grandmother, who called me first thing. She told me what had happened in a cold, emotionless voice that I recognized as shock. I told her who I would call, so she wouldn't have to call those people. I told her I'd be on a flight as soon as possible to support her. And I was. I flew in the next day, in fix-it mode once again. My grandma needed someone to take care of her. She had lost her husband, and now her son. And I was going to make everything better.

But when I got there, I found a different story. Grandma didn't need support. She told me she was an "old Catholic lady" and knew her way around a funeral, even if my father was a Baptist. She also had my uncle, her friends, my father's friends, and so many others offering support. My younger brothers, though, they needed more support than I had ever imagined.

I sat, listening to one brother, and then another, and then another, as they told me what they had seen. The shock and dread when they heard the gunshot. It was a hard neighborhood they lived in, and they knew exactly what a gunshot sounded like. They described finding him with a hole in his chest, still bleeding.

Internally, I was horrified. I retreated. I gave hugs and told people what I thought they needed to hear, so long as it was true. I gave more hugs and cooked dinner. I listened to my grandmother talk about her son with his friends as they stopped by, and with her siblings as they called to offer condolences. Somewhere in here, I realized I was back in that aching, throbbing numbness. I was lost all over again, and I didn't know why.

At the funeral, I had already prepared myself for people to be kind, to offer condolences, to think that I, his oldest kid who was named after him, would have had a relationship with him. I was prepared to thank everyone for coming, and thank them for sharing their stories, since they all knew him better than I did. What I wasn't prepared for was the raw, heart-wrenching truths that surfaced.

My father was a racist. There's no way to soften that ugly truth. He wouldn't allow a person of color to touch him, even. This was a painful truth for me as a kid, because most of the people I knew were themselves people of color, and I couldn't bring my friends over, or introduce my parents to theirs. Everyone, and I mean everyone, knew my father was a racist. But right in the middle of the funeral, a small Black lady stood. The silence that fell on the service was thick enough to chew. She took a deep breath, and then told a story of heroism, selflessness, gentility, and savagery that I couldn't believe until my grandmother later confirmed it.

This lady—who left before I could introduce myself—shared the story of her daughter being attacked by a dog. I don't know what prompted the attack, but I learned that the girl was very young, five or six years old. The dog was a large mixed breed stray. My father saw the dog attack and sprinted at the both of them. He wrestled with the dog, pull its jaws open, and freed the little girl from the dog's bite. He sustained several injuries as he was bit and scratched in the process. I don't know what happened to the dog. But this lady told us that her baby girl would have died if he hadn't intervened.

For the first time in the several days since my father's death, I experienced a true sense of loss. It struck me as a fundamental truth that I would never actually know my father. That I, in fact, never knew him at all. I was 23 years old and didn't know even the basic truths of who my father was as a person, and now all I had to work with was other people's memories of him. It felt like whiplash. Was I there because it was my job, as his oldest kid, to see things done? Or was I there for the reason everyone else was: To grieve the loss of a person with immutable value?

When the funeral home played "Blackbird" by the Beatles, I cried for the first time. One tiny tear, and a burning sensation in my face. I did my best to listen to everyone else speak. I thanked everyone for coming and sending my father off with love. I helped my father's third wife sort his belongings to give away. I ate, and slept, and gave hugs. I flew home the next day.

The next few months were a blur of emotional revelations. Each of these was precipitated by a sense of grief and followed by (perhaps overly dramatic) changes in my life.

When my father died, I was enrolled in college to get a degree in nursing. I was working in an emergency department as part of my education. Not long after my father's funeral, we had an infant die. I had to leave work, and I never worked in a hospital again.

I went on a trip with friends, and I was the only person who wasn't able to bring their partner. My partner was busy, so I went without him. Seeing the loving, caring, and profoundly healthy relationships on display that week drove home how unhappy I was in my relationship. When I got home, I tried to work things out. Within a month, we had broken up, and I moved over a thousand miles away.

Unfortunately, the geographic cure doesn't actually help emotional problems. My grief, the sadness and pain and fear—everything—followed me to my new home. I realized I was afraid of dying like my father, and that for the first time, I actually believed I could die. It felt like too much. I felt like I was drowning in a world where I was the only person who didn't know how to handle my emotions.

I was actually, truly grieving for the first time, and I couldn't stay in that space. I also didn't know how to get past it. What I did know, is that somewhere ahead of me were infinite timelines, and in all of them, I died. In too many of them, I died by suicide because everything was too much to handle alone.

So, I did the last thing I expected myself to do. I went to a doctor and told them my brain was broken and asked for help. I did so knowing that the people I had lost, many of whom aren't mentioned here, all wanted me to be happy, and to be my best self. I also knew that none of them would hold it against me for asking for help.

I got a therapist. Then I got a psychiatrist. Then I got a few hospitalizations while I figured out my medications. When I met my wife, I tried to scare her away with all these labels the doctors had given me. PTSD, bipolar disorder, panic attacks, depression, anxiety, OCD. She smiled at me and said, "Okay." And I remembered my friends, and my grandparents, and my father, and how often they had taken me as I am, right now. I started to actually believe it *would* be okay.

Most importantly, I began a new grieving process. I grieved for the immortal life I had deluded myself into thinking I was entitled to. It's a natural delusion, with an evolutionary basis. If you think you will never die, you keep trying. But somehow, I learned how to stay invested while recognizing that I would die one day. I went through a lot of therapists. I have had a lot of doctors. So many times, I thought I was wasting my time, that this couldn't be the right thing. So many times, I was wrong. I learned how to grieve. I learned how to love, and cherish, and do things that matter.

Ultimately, I learned that the Southern way of handling emotions doesn't work. "Push it down," "Crying is ugly," "Emotions are weakness," and so many other stereotypes I had internalized were only causing me harm. I learned candor—the ability to tell the truth openly, without holding back. I learned that my wife respects me for who I am, and my kids have a healthier relationship with their emotional health because they've been able to see me talking about— and working through—my emotions. Some of this I was able to accept right away, but it took longer to internalize it. Other things took years before I was able to pin down a particular emotion, label it, and understand what causes it.

Today, I teach Dialectical Behavioral Therapy. I attend individual therapy every week. I support people who are grieving by having honest, candid conversations with them. And I have those conversations with people who aren't grieving, but who will be one day. Because I've finally accepted the truth that death is not just possible for everyone. Rather, it is guaranteed for everyone. But I've also accepted that the knowledge of that eventual death gives me the power to be my best and most authentic self every day.

Hopefully, when I die, I won't have any regrets. And that's not an idle hope—it's something I work toward every day. I work to let go of the past, I allow the future to come to me, and I take this moment, this timeline, and I wring every ounce of emotion from it, no matter what that emotion is. The reason why? Because I now know that every emotion has a job. Every feeling, reaction, thought, urge, and even action has underlying factors that shape my life. I also know I can change those factors by doing the work.

Finally, I know that by changing those factors, I can take control of my life, my future, and my decisions.

Grief is usually the story of endings, but for me, it was the catalyst to a lifetime of new beginnings, and a new version of myself. It's a tool, nothing more, nothing less.

About the Author

Rory Bristol is a queer non-binary writer and mental health educator. Rory is a member of the Partner Advisory Counsel for the local community mental health center, where he meets with the leadership team monthly to help guide their care practice to a more accessible, equitable, and just system that serves everyone in the community. He is also the creator of UpRoryUs, a mental health education channel on YouTube.com, where he teaches therapy skills, anatomy, biology, psychology, and sociology in the effort to provide a free tool anyone can use to improve their own health. Find his work at rorybristol.com.

"Everybody knows they're going to die, but nobody believes it. If we did, we would do things differently." - Morrie Schwartz

Echoes

By Steve Lenker

Grief echoes.

Grief is the lingering loss that replaces the thing lost. Grief is the tombstone that comes and stays after the thing is done. It falls to the erosion of time, but only slowly, the way wind and rain carve little rivulets into stone that dissolve it into nothing as ages pass.

We can feel grief over so many things. Great or small; vague or clear and specific as crystal; a person, an object, or a circumstance—grief is strewn throughout existence. That is a human fact, the price we pay for the capacity to feel joy. But for those of us who live with the repeating echoes of old pain, moving past grief does not happen in a day, or a week, or a year. Our grief fades, but not in a way that we can easily notice. It tiptoes away, blocking the sun less with time, but never seeming to.

Of course, grief has its hierarchies. Grief runs the gamut from the vanishing of a minor, pleasant situation or trifling physical object—the equivalent of a dust speak—to the Sisyphean boulder of the loss of a loved one. The common element is the echo of the loss.

It seems ridiculous to use the word "grief" to label your reaction to the smallest losses. If asked, we would shy away from the word and substitute "annoyance" or "irritation". And in fact, our regret doesn't usually last very long at all. But it does last longer than you would think it should if it echoes in your head.

For many of us who are neurodivergent, small losses are not the trifles that neurotypicals would find them to be. Even the malfunction of a favorite pen, the discontinuance of a precise brand of food at a grocery store, or the cancellation of a television show can bring us difficulties. If you combine such failures of the world around us with the mental echoes that give them longevity, you might be more inclined to accept the word "grief" for your reaction.

"Grief" describes your experience better as the scale of the loss increases. Suppose you are fired or laid off. Of course this affects everyone badly, but we neurodivergent people are known to have difficulties finding work. Add the effect of the echoes in your mind, and the grief can be considerable. To this day, some of us have to wrestle with the consequences of jobs that ended years or even decades ago.

Naturally, for most of us, the greatest grief arises from the loss of loved ones, human or animal. The owners of cats and dogs can relate especially well to the latter. We might miss beloved pets for the rest of our lives, even if we knew them in childhood. Their faces, their sounds, their endearing behaviors—these are the building blocks of the echoes that resound throughout our lives when we survive them.

The loss of human beings inspires even more echoes. Bear in mind, of course, that losses of people do not always occur through death. So often, they simply leave. They might have perfectly good reasons, but so very often, we can't see this. We might realize that our lives improve with their departure, or we might not. In a perfect storm of grief of this kind, we blame ourselves for not measuring up to the person who leaves. Some sort of personal failing on our part must be responsible, and the search for that deadly flaw can give rise to lifelong echoes of grief.

Now we have arrived at the summit of the hierarchy of grief, at least for most of us—the grief when a loved one dies. This is in a sense the highest and purest form of grief, because unlike the others, the object of the grief can never truly be replaced. Only time makes a dent in this grief, and often we are not left with enough time in our lives to truly heal from the loss of the one we mourn.

Grief of this kind can reshape our lives as few things can. We grow with our loved ones, intertwine with them—and their departure can leave us with a limp. We compensate for the limp, learn to adjust for it, but it might never completely go away.

So how does the grief of neurodivergent people differ from the grief of others at this level?

As in all things, it depends on the neurodivergent person. Neurodivergence is like a fingerprint; generalizations about us can only go so far. Your neurodivergence is not mine, and your grief is not mine.

I can only tell you about my grief.

In fact, I already have.

Grief echoes.

Since I graduated from high school, I have lost four family members. I am now almost sixty, older than three of the four when they died. Two of those three committed suicide.

All four echo to me. They echo in different ways, with different feelings and nuances.

My father, who died at the age of eighty-three, echoes to me. Unlike the others, a large part of his echo involves a sense of completion. He lived a long, full life, and it was not cut short.

The other three were all younger than fifty when they died. One died in a car accident; two committed suicide, as I said. Absolutely they all echo. The suicide victims in particular give forth echoes that cry out for the help that they should have received. They were casualties of one force or another; their lives *were* cut short.

Perhaps not even loved ones represent the greatest depths of grief that we experience. For a few of us, the true source of grief is societal. We pine for a world that believes in and practices social justice. In its absence, we find ourselves surrounded by the pain and waste of the millions whom our rulers do not treat as they deserve to be treated. Of this, too, we neurodivergent people might be more keenly aware than most.

This grief, too, echoes.

About the Author

Steve is a neurodivergent digital artist who lives on a homestead in the Ozarks populated by horses, chickens, cats, and a variety of wildlife, many of which show up in his art. His love of science fiction and space shines in his work, which often depicts vistas from other planets, but often with familiar subjects. He is the author of the fantasy novella *Source of the Third*, and hard at work on more creative endeavors.

Website: https://stevelenker.net

About the Publisher

Epona Muse Publishing seeks to lift marginalized voices in anthologies that inform, entertain, and question the current paradigm. For more information about current published works and future projects, please visit EponaMuse.com

Facebook: https://facebook.com/eponaauthor
Twitter: https://twitter.com/eponaauthor
Instagram: https://instagram.com/eponaauthorsolutions
YouTube: https://youtube.com/@eponaauthor